# The Invitation

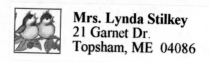
# The Invitation

### THE
### NOT-SO-SIMPLE TRUTH
### ABOUT FOLLOWING
### JESUS

## GREG SIDDERS

Revell

a division of Baker Publishing Group
Grand Rapids, Michigan

© 2011 by Greg Sidders

Published by Revell
a division of Baker Publishing Group
P.O. Box 6287, Grand Rapids, MI 49516-6287
www.revellbooks.com

Printed in the United States of America

Library of Congress Cataloging-in-Publication Data
Sidders, Greg, 1961–
    The invitation : the not-so-simple truth about following Jesus / Greg Sidders.
       p.   cm.
    Includes bibliographical references (p.   ).
    ISBN 978-0-8007-3403-9 (pbk.)
    1. Christian life—Biblical teaching. 2. Jesus Christ—Teachings. I. Title.
BS2417.C5S53  2011
248.4—dc22                                                    2010044382

11   12   13   14   15   16   17        7   6   5   4   3   2   1

To
Sean, Brian, and Kyle,
disciples of Jesus

# Contents

# Introduction

Soon after I decided to follow Jesus, I started avoiding him at all costs.

I want to tell you how it happened, because I think you might recognize your own story in mine.

I was a sophomore in college, living in a godless dormitory and dabbling in its multiple choices. But two things kept me from enjoying myself: anxiety about death and proximity to Bob, the Christian on my floor who always abstained but never judged.

One day in the dining commons, Bob walked past me with his food tray, stopped, and said, "I'd like to come by your room tonight. There's something I want to talk to you about."

"Uh, okay." I could not imagine what he wanted to talk about.

It turned out to be the most important conversation of my life. He shared with me the secret of immortality. The simple truth that Jesus died for me so that I could live forever was something I had never heard in church. It spoke to my deepest need and most paralyzing fear—and yet I stubbornly rejected it. "I pray every day," I said to Bob, "and I don't think God is going to send me to hell just because I don't have Jesus as my go-between."

Rather than argue with me, Bob said, "Well, since you pray every day, why don't you ask God if he thinks you need Jesus?"

I didn't see any harm in that, so after Bob left, I prayed. "God, I know I don't need Jesus, but if you think I do, tell me." I repeated the same prayer a couple dozen times over the next several weeks. I didn't hear any heavenly voice, so I concluded that God agreed with me.

It was long after I stopped asking that God answered. I was lying in bed late at night when I did hear a voice—not with my ears but with my heart: *Greg, you have been running away from me long enough. Now, turn around and follow me.*

I cannot explain how I knew it was the voice of Jesus (any more than you could explain the times God has spoken to you), but I knew. I responded pretty much like I did when Bob invited himself to my dorm room. "Uh, okay."

In an instant a flash flood of joy engulfed me. I knew, with the certainty that only the Spirit of God can give, that I was going to live forever.

And the exhilaration lingered. I joined an on-campus Christian group, made new friends, and bought my first Bible, one with the words of Christ in red.

And then I did something that turned my euphoria into vertigo. I read the words in red.

"Hate your father and mother."

"Take up your cross."

"Do good to those who hate you."

"Sell your possessions."

"Be slave of all."

I discovered that this man who called me to follow him was a radical. Either that or (please, dear God) I had purchased a defective Bible. I borrowed my friends' Bibles and compared them to mine. Sure enough, theirs said the same thing. I pointed to Jesus's most shocking statements and asked them, "Have you read this?"

"Uh-huh," they would yawn.

I couldn't understand why they weren't as appalled as I was. It was unthinkable to me to actually do what Jesus said. And yet I wanted to be a Christian (because I wanted to go to heaven). So I did the only sensible thing: I skipped the words in red. Well, not all of them, but if they got too upsetting, I simply picked up where the black ink resumed. I had wonderful devotions in the Epistles of Paul during this time.

Then one day a simple question popped into my mind: *How can I call myself a Christian if I don't follow Christ?*

That was when I made an apprehensive reentry into the red zone. Soon afterward, I read the words of Jesus in Matthew 11:28–30: "Come to me, all you who are weary and burdened, and I will give you rest. Take my yoke upon you and learn from me, for I am gentle and humble in heart, and you will find rest for your souls. For my yoke is easy and my burden is light."

Maybe I should have been comforted by those words, but I wasn't. I was confused. How could Jesus call the yoke that to me seemed so hard "easy"? How could he say that the burden I found so heavy was really "light"? At the heart of Christ's invitation is the verb *learn.* If you were to open a Greek New Testament to Matthew 11:29, you would see the word *mathete.* It's a verb that comes from the same root as the noun *mathetes*, which we translate "disciple." Jesus said that being his disciple is *easy* and *light*.

Seriously? Have you read those passages in which Jesus describes what his disciples do? There are seven of them in the Gospels—so, yes, I suppose they are light in volume and easy to memorize, but on the commitment scale, they are among the heaviest statements Jesus ever made. So where is the ease and lightness Jesus promised?

It's in the doing of what we find daunting.

I have discovered—or, I should say, I am discovering—that the teachings of Jesus seem hard and heavy until I actually do them. That's when I say, "Well, that wasn't so bad. In fact, I've never felt better." Once I penetrate the ominous mirage, I break through to the soul-rest I long for. Those passages that used to intimidate me have become precious to me, and I cannot imagine reverting to a mild version of Christianity with all the hard sayings of Jesus edited out. How hollow that would be.

Might you use that word—hollow—to describe your Christian experience? If so, could Christ-avoidance be the cause? Is it possible that you have been either frightened away by his most revolutionary teachings or insulated from them by tidy evangelical theology? What might happen if you were to take a fresh, unfiltered look at the discipleship sayings of Jesus? What if you read the Gospels as if the rest of the New Testament didn't exist? Because, remember, it didn't exist during the ministry of Jesus. What if you had to deal with Jesus on his own terms?

If you're up for it, I'd like to take you back in time, back before the cross mopped up our messes, before the resurrection released the superhuman power of the Spirit, before the apostles helped clarify what Jesus left fuzzy. How I thank God for the cross, the resurrection, and the apostles, but something precious is lost when we reverse the order of things. It's like reading the last chapter first. When we encounter the teachings of Jesus chronologically, in the order they were given, the transformation is deeper. At least that has been true in my life.

So let's go back to the beginning—back to Jesus unplugged. Let's zoom in on those passages that include phrases like "Follow me" and "my disciples." As you consider the implications of being a disciple of Jesus, you'll invariably wrestle with the same questions I have wrestled with: *Did Jesus really mean that? Could I really do that? What are my other options?* But, as you take the risk of bearing his yoke, you'll discover that quality of life that everybody seeks but only disciples find.

Let me give you the invitation in the form of a visual image that was given to me fifteen years after I first heard Jesus say to me, "Follow me." I had just finished watching a three-hour dramatization of the Gospel of Matthew called *The Visual Bible*. It was on videotape (I know, I am dating myself), and when the screen faded to black, I thought it was over. But it wasn't. Right before the credits, there is a thirty-second, silent, slow-motion shot of Jesus walking along the Sea of Galilee. It begins with a close-up of his sandaled feet, and then it gradually widens to show him walking away from the camera. Suddenly, Jesus stops, looks toward the camera, and, with a slight smile and a beckoning gesture, invites the viewer to follow him. He turns away and continues to walk, then stops again, turns around, and, with a broad smile on his face, waves his arm as if to say, "Come on!" Then the picture freezes for several seconds.

Can you see it? I replayed the videotape so many times I wore it out. (No worries, I replaced it with a DVD.) I'll never forget the scene. Especially the smile. It's as if Jesus couldn't conceal the joy he felt in knowing what was in store for those who follow him. If I had still been a new Christian, sweating my way through the Gospels for the first time, I might have interpreted his grin as sadistic, but after fifteen years of following him, that smile brought tears to my eyes—tears of joy, gratitude, and affection toward this man, this God, whom I once feared but now loved with all my heart.

You want to follow Jesus, don't you? It's why you picked up this book. It's why you're still reading. And it's why, by the time we finish this turbulent, exhilarating journey together, you will be more certain than ever that it is in running to Jesus, not from him, that we find the life we were created to live.

---

**A Word about the Study Guide**

The study guide in the back of this book has both "Before" and "After" sections for each chapter. If you want to study the Scriptures on your own before you read my thoughts on them, the "Before" sections will help you to do that. If you would like to reflect on or discuss with others the practical implications of each chapter's content, use the "After" sections.

---

# 1

## Letting Go

WHAT'S KEEPING YOU
FROM FOLLOWING JESUS?

Follow me."

It's not a command you can obey sitting down. That's easy to miss when you read it in the Bible because—well, because generally when you read it you're sitting down. But when Jesus spoke these words to the first disciples, he was always standing—and rarely standing still. In order to follow, you had to get up and go.

Philip was the first one Jesus summoned. John 1:43 says that Jesus found Philip, which implies that he went looking for him. He did not pick Philip randomly; he singled him out. Imagine it. A man you hardly know approaches you and speaks all of two words: "Follow me." What do you do? Most people would go, all right, but in the opposite direction. But for some reason, Philip followed.

Simon and Andrew were next. Jesus was walking along the shore of the Sea of Galilee. He saw the two fishermen casting a net into the lake. "Come, follow me," he said to them, "and I will make you fishers of men" (Matt. 4:19). How long did it take them to decide? Not long. "At once they left their nets and followed him" (Matt. 4:20).

They got as far as the next boat. There were James and John. Jesus beckoned them, and "immediately they left the boat and their father and followed him" (Matt. 4:22).

A short time later, as Jesus was walking along, he saw a tax collector by the name of Levi sitting at his collection booth. "Follow me," Jesus said to him, and that was all it took. "Levi got up, left everything and followed him" (Luke 5:28).

In each case, the response was immediate, unconditional, and ambulatory. They got up and went. Why would anyone in their right mind leave everything behind to follow this man, not knowing where he was going?

## Why Follow Jesus?

The easy answer is that Jesus was God, and God doesn't take no for an answer. But that's not it, because some people did say no to Jesus. His authority was not irresistible.

No, there was more to it than who Jesus was. There was also what he offered. And what was that? A better future. That's why people follow Jesus—because they believe that whatever he has in store for them is better than what they leave behind.

Take Levi, for example. Tax collecting was a dirty business, and even though it paid well, it left Levi feeling empty and unredeemable. But then he heard of this man, Jesus, who was going around forgiving sins, as if he were God, and healing, because he actually was God. *If only he could forgive someone as far gone as me*, Levi thought. *I'd give anything to get a second chance*. But the reverie was fleeting, because he knew the chances were remote.

And then, suddenly, there he was. Jesus. Looking at Levi, of all people, and saying, "I want you." It was a once-in-a-lifetime opportunity to start fresh, with a clean slate. It was the pearl of great price, worth more than all the money in the world. Uprooting was the easiest thing Levi ever did, because what he left behind was rubbish; it was dung compared to the surpassing greatness of knowing the man who forgives sins. It's easy for people to follow Jesus when they are eager to shed their past.

But what if you're happy with where life has taken you? What if you have a clear conscience and a comfortable lifestyle? Jesus calls people like that to follow him too. What's the draw for somebody whose roots are deep in enviable soil?

That was Simon's story. Matthew and Mark cut to the chase: Jesus called him, and he came. But Luke and John fill in the blanks. They explain why Simon was willing to drop his nets and start walking. It wasn't because of wanderlust. He had the companionship of a wife and family, the security of a stable job, and the luxury of a home. He was living the Israeli dream. He thought, "It doesn't get any better than this."

Then Jesus showed up and said, "Oh yes it does."

It didn't start on the day Jesus called Simon, but sometime earlier. Perhaps it was at the end of a typical workday, when Simon was unwinding at home, that his brother Andrew burst through the door and announced, "We have found the Messiah!" Andrew had always been the more spiritual of the two, so Simon gave him an I'm-glad-it-works-for-you nod. But Andrew pestered him until he agreed to go and meet Jesus.

When Simon arrived at the place where Jesus was staying, John 1:42 says that "Jesus looked at him," but that's a mild translation. Literally, he *gazed* at Simon. Tell me that wouldn't give you the willies.

And then Jesus spoke. "You are Simon son of John." Weird. How did he know his name? Then he did something even more odd. He renamed him. "You will be called Rocky." *Cephas*, which is Aramaic for *Petros*, which is Greek for *Rock*.

Now, if you know anything about Simon, you know that he was not a rock-like guy. Stable, consistent, level-headed, dependable? No. If Jesus had chosen a name that described the kind of man Simon was at that time, he would have said, "You will be called Flakey." But instead he named him prophetically, foretelling what kind of man Simon would become under his influence. Those first words out of Jesus's mouth touched a nerve in Simon's soul. Jesus said to Simon, essentially, "Follow me, and I will transform you into the kind of person you never dreamed you would be."

Would that mess with your head? A stranger who others say is anointed by God stares at you, calls you by name, and says, "I know who you are and who you have the potential to be. And I intend to help you become the best possible version of yourself."

It rattled Simon, but not enough to inspire instant allegiance. He returned home—back to the familiar, safe rut of his routine. But those disturbing, alluring words of Jesus echoed in his mind and aroused a yearning deep inside, at that subterranean level that so many of us leave unexplored. It was foreign territory for Simon, so he didn't go there. He tried to forget that man, that gaze, that voice, those words.

## Jesus the Unavoidable

But Jesus can be persistent. Matthew 4:13 says, "Leaving Nazareth, he went and lived in Capernaum." What a coincidence. That just happened to be Simon's neighborhood.

We don't know how long Jesus was in Capernaum before Simon agreed with Andrew that Jesus was the Messiah, but eventually he came around. Yet Simon exercised his faith from a safe distance, as an observer rather than as a participant. He was a back-row disciple.

That all changed on the day Jesus decided to preach on the beach, near the fishermen who had docked their boats on the shore of the Sea of Galilee. When the crowd grew so large that Jesus was literally backed into the water, he climbed into one of the boats. Guess which one? "The one belonging to Simon," Luke 5:3 tells us. Like a heat-seeking missile, Jesus was closing in on his target.

He asked—who else?—Simon to get in and skipper the boat. After it was a little offshore, Jesus sat down and taught the people. I doubt Simon was listening. He was probably thinking, *Why is this man stalking me?*

When Jesus finished teaching, Simon quickly started rowing, eager to get ashore before Jesus could do anything that might humiliate him in front of his friends. But it was no use. Jesus said to him (why do I imagine a smile on his face?), "Put out into deep water, and let down the nets for a catch" (Luke 5:4).

Awkward. The preacher tells the fisherman to go fishing, in the heat of the day, when—as any fisherman worth his salt knows—the fish are too deep for the nets to catch. The best fishing was always done at night, and Simon was quick to inform the Son of God of that fact. "Master, we've worked hard all night and haven't caught anything." And then there was a pause, just long enough for Simon's brain to catch up with his mouth. *Who am I to argue with Jesus?* he thought. *I'm a fisherman, that's who. He may know how to preach—oh yeah, and heal people—but I know how to fish. Still, he's the Master. But this doesn't make any sense.* Back and forth his mind raced. Finally, reluctantly, he surrendered. "But because you say so, I will let down the nets."

He summoned his crew as the crowd on the beach snickered. Out they rowed, and down went the nets. Simon's face was red with embarrassment and anger.

But not for long. Suddenly the nets were full. As the men struggled to haul them in, they began to tear under the weight. A second boat was summoned. Both boats were loaded so full of fish that they began to sink.

Simon was undone. Luke says that he fell at Jesus's knees. Why not at his feet? Because they were knee-deep in fish. That was as low as Simon could go. Facedown on top of the flopping pile, Simon cried, "Go away from me, Lord; I am a sinful man!" What was his sin? Unbelief: "For he and all his companions were astonished at the catch of fish they had taken" (Luke 5:8–9).

But if there was anything Simon should have known by then, it was Jesus had no intention of going away—at least, not without inviting him to come along. Jesus said to Simon, "Don't be afraid. From now on you will catch people" (Luke

5:10 NIrV). Don't just read the text; observe the subtext. How many people? As many as those two boats full of fish! "Simon," Jesus was saying, "it's my plan, not only to change your character, but also to use you to change the destiny of countless others."

That was the offer Simon couldn't refuse. Personal transformation was one thing, but being used by Jesus to help people live forever—how do you say no to that?

## A Personal Invitation

Would you say yes if Jesus pursued you with as much determination as he pursued Simon Peter? I have news for you: He is. It's no accident that you are reading these words right now. And soon we'll come to passages where Jesus will offer you the same future he offered Simon—a future of personal transformation and eternal impact.

But if that's the future you want, there's one thing you're going to have to do right at the outset. You're going to have to get up and go. And that means leaving something behind, doesn't it? It may be your family, your home, or your career. It may be a bank account or a prized possession. It may be your reputation, your pride, or your safety. It may be a lifelong dream. Whatever it is, if you want a better future, you're going to have to do what Simon and Andrew and James and John did. "They pulled their boats up on shore, left everything and followed [Jesus]" (Luke 5:11).

Seven years ago, I was in the same Bible study group as a high school math teacher named Heather. Teaching is a great way to serve Jesus, but he had something else in mind for Heather. Over time we learned that she felt a strong calling to be a missionary—specifically, a Bible translator. Do you know where Bible translators live? In remote tribes. Heather was up for that, but she wanted to do one thing first: marry a man who wanted to go with her. She had dreamed of being a wife and mom long before she dreamed of being a missionary. Common sense told her to wait, but Jesus was telling her to get up and go.

She cried every night for months. She purposely laid on her back in bed, facing the ceiling, so that God could look down from heaven and see the agony she was going through. Finally, excruciatingly, she left her dream behind and followed Jesus. She quit her job, joined a mission organization, and moved from the West Coast to the Deep South to take linguistics classes in preparation for deployment.

On the first day of orientation, Heather met David, who had come from the East Coast. He too had surrendered his desire to marry before becoming a missionary. A month later they were dating. A year and a half after that, they were married. And now they are living in the Middle East, working with others to translate the Bible into multiple dialects, so that people who have never before read the book that contains the secret of eternal life can do so in their native language. And, by the way, David and Heather have three children, with a fourth on the way.

"I tell you the truth," Jesus said in Luke 18:29–30, "no one who has left home or wife or brothers or parents or children for the sake of the kingdom of God will fail to receive many times as much in this age and, in the age to come, eternal life." Jesus does not invite us to follow him so that he can ruin our lives. He does it to give us more than we could ask or imagine.

Who doesn't want that? The rub is, we want to follow Jesus without leaving anything behind—let alone everything.

## Traveling Light

"I will follow you wherever you go," a man announced to Jesus in Luke 9:57.

Really? "Foxes have holes and birds of the air have nests, but the Son of Man has no place to lay his head" (Luke 9:58). "Are you willing to be homeless? Rootless? Mobile?" Apparently not. We never hear of that man again.

Jesus said to another man exactly what he had said to Simon Peter: "Follow me" (Luke 9:59).

The man was willing to go, just not right away. "Lord, first let me go and bury my father" (Luke 9:59). His dad probably wasn't dead yet, but just as soon as he did die, as soon as the man's family obligations were fulfilled and his inheritance banked, he would jump to his feet and go. "Jesus, you can be the Lord of everything but my timetable."

Jesus said to him, "Let the dead bury their own dead, but you go and proclaim the kingdom of God." Nowhere in the Gospels does Jesus wait for anybody. It's now or never.

Still another said, "I will follow you, Lord; but first let me go back and say good-bye to my family" (Luke 9:61). "Let me go home and weep with them over the sacrifices I will make. Let me go and reminisce about the good old days, and grieve the fact that I have to leave those I love to follow you."

Jesus replied, "No one who puts his hand to the plow and looks back is fit for service in the kingdom of God" (Luke 9:62). "If you're going to regret following me, just stay home."

Tragically, most do. It's not that we don't want to follow Jesus, it's just that we want to do it sitting down. We ask him to stay. He tells us to go. And whether the rest of your life turns out to be ordinary or extraordinary may just boil down to this one question: Which do you want more—what Jesus offers, or what you have to leave behind to get it?

# 2

# The Leap of Faith

## WHAT HAPPENS WHEN YOU DO
## WHAT JESUS SAYS?

Some time ago I met the founder of a ministry called Summit Expedition. "What do you do?" I asked him.

"We provide adventure-based educational experiences."

"I see," I said. But I really didn't. So I asked him to give me an example.

"We take our clients to the top of a cliff, harness them to rock-climbing ropes, and tell them to rappel down the cliff. When they back off the side of the cliff and put all their weight on the ropes, they have an adventure-based educational experience about the meaning of faith."

I had two thoughts: *What a great idea!* and *Glad I'll never have to do it.*

Little did I know that one day I would have my own adventure-based educational experience, thanks to a ropes course in the mountains of Southern California. If you've never experienced this, just imagine climbing very high, trying not to fall, and failing, and you'll get the idea.

It's actually quite safe. At least that's what our instructor told us when he was strapping us into rope harnesses before we headed up the mountain. "This rope can hold ten times your body weight," he said, "and there will always be someone at the other end of the rope who is strong enough to hold you up, even if you fall." I believed him, and I felt safe.

Then we took a short hike, and I saw something that made me feel unsafe. It was a wooden power pole, just like the kind that support electric wires in suburban neighborhoods. It rose from earth to sky, parallel to the pine trees that surrounded it. But whereas the trees had limbs, the pole had nothing but tiny wooden nubs, protruding just enough to give climbers a toehold. A sign was displayed next to the pole: "The Leap of Faith."

Our first challenge was simply to climb the pole until we were standing on the top of it. *No problem*, I thought. *It's not that high. And, besides, what's the worst that can happen? My rope will hold me up.*

But somehow, the pole miraculously tripled in height as I was climbing it. When I got to the top, I was in the fetal position, hugging the pole for dear life. Finally I mustered the courage to stand up straight. I looked down. Bad idea. The pole was swaying in the wind. I began to exhale as if blowing into a tuba.

But climbing the pole was only half the challenge. Hanging about ten feet in front of me was a trapeze. The only way to get to it was by taking The Leap. If I missed the bar, nothing would keep me from plunging to certain death except the skinny little rope clipped to my backside. At that moment, I understood the concept of faith as never before.

I considered my options. I could either crawl back down the pole in utter humiliation, or I could take The Leap. More out of pride than courage, I jumped. My fingertips touched the trapeze, but I couldn't hold on. Suddenly I was falling, face-first and fast . . . but only for an instant. Almost immediately I felt the tension of the rope and I began to float, slowly and softly, to the ground.

What a rush! I had utterly abandoned myself to the rope, and in taking that leap of faith, I felt so much more alive than I would have if I had chosen to play it safe.

But let's say I did play it safe. Let's say I stood at the bottom of the pole and the instructor asked me, "Do you believe the rope is strong enough to hold you up?"

"Of course," I said. "You yourself told me it could hold ten times my body weight."

"Do you really believe that?"

"Absolutely."

"Well, then how about climbing that pole and taking the Leap of Faith?"

Long pause. "Well, no, I don't think I'm quite ready to do that."

If I said I believed in the rope but opted out of the jump, would my faith in the rope be genuine?

## Fake Faith

What if the object of my faith was not a rope but a teacher? What if that teacher gave me a whole new set of rules to play by, and said, "Live my way and you'll experience life as it was meant to be"? And what if I said, "I believe in this teacher"—but I didn't do what he told me to do? Would my faith in him be genuine? And should I expect to experience the quality of life he promised?

The teacher, of course, is Jesus. And the scenario I have just described is all too common. There are many more people who say they believe in him than there are people who actually do what he says.

It has been this way from the beginning. When Jesus first exploded onto the scene, his compassionate love, miraculous power, and novel teachings attracted "believers" like a magnet attracts iron filings. John 8:30 describes the typical response to his ministry: "Even as he spoke, many put their faith in him."

But did they really? There was only one way to tell. "To the Jews who had believed him, Jesus said, 'If you hold to my teaching, you are really my disciples'" (John 8:31).

That's the test. Do you believe in Jesus enough to put the full weight of your life on the rope of his words? Do you believe in him enough to jump off the pole of life-as-you've-always-lived-it into the free fall of life-as-Jesus-teaches-you-to-live-it?

If you're not aware of any gap between how you are living and how you know Jesus wants you to live, that may be an abstract question. But if there is any area of your life in which you know your behavior clashes with Jesus's teaching, it's a disturbingly concrete one: *Am I willing to surrender this area of my life to him?*

Instinctively, we answer that question with this one: *Why should I?*

And if we don't get a compelling answer, we'll never take the leap. So Jesus gives us an answer. He stands under the trapeze, if you will, and tells us why we should jump.

## The Leap to Certainty

First, he says, it is the only way to be sure he is worthy of our trust. "If you hold to my teaching, you are really my disciples. *Then you will know the truth*" (John 8:31–32).

The word Jesus uses for "know" is not intellectual knowledge; it is experiential knowledge. It's deep-down, rock-solid, beyond-a-shadow-of-a-doubt assurance.

There are many different religions in the world. How do you know you chose the right one? How do you know that Jesus is the best teacher of truth, rather than Mohammed, or Buddha, or Confucius? And how do you know that Jesus can be trusted, not just to get you to heaven, but also to give you the best possible life on earth? Simple: Jump.

You see, the certainty we want comes not before we decide to follow Jesus but as a result of following Jesus. Before I jumped off the power pole, I *believed* the rope could hold me up. But when I jumped, I *knew* it could. In the same way, you cannot be certain that Jesus is the way and the truth and the life until you obey his teachings with no-going-back abandonment.

The faith of many Christians is not joyful certainty but anxious hope. They're not 100 percent sure that Jesus is the right one to follow, but they have their fingers crossed. Others don't wrestle with doubts. They just know. Why? Because they have taken the risk of doing what Jesus taught, and his faithfulness has made their faith unshakeable.

If someone in the John 8 crowd of "believers" had asked Simon Peter if he *knew* the truth, what do you think he would have said?

I'll give you a hint. Jesus spoke these words sometime after he and Peter walked on water. Before that stormy night, Peter was among the disciples of little faith who sat in the boat and said of Jesus, "What kind of man is this?" (Matt. 8:27). But when Jesus invited Peter to get out of the boat and walk on water, everything changed. Sure, Peter ended up wet and humiliated, and Jesus did say to him, "You of little faith . . . why did you doubt?" (Matt. 14:31). But what happened the next day? Jesus delivered a sermon that was so shocking that "many of his disciples turned back and no longer followed him" (John 6:66). As disciples were leaving in droves, Jesus turned to the twelve apostles and said, "You do not want to leave too, do you?" (John 6:67).

Guess who spoke up? Simon Peter. "Lord, to whom shall we go? You have the words of eternal life. We believe *and know* that you are the Holy One of God" (John 6:68–69). The word Peter used for "know" is the very same word that Jesus used when he said, "You will *know* the truth." It is certainty rooted in experience. That's what we get when we hold to Christ's teaching.

But it's not all we get.

### The Leap to Freedom

"If you hold to my teaching, you are really my disciples. Then you will know the truth, and *the truth will set you free*" (John 8:31–32).

30

Free? Free from what? That's exactly what "the Jews who had believed in him" wondered. "They answered him, 'We are Abraham's descendants and have never been slaves of anyone. How can you say that we shall be set free?' Jesus replied, 'I tell you the truth, everyone who sins is a slave to sin. . . . So if the Son sets you free, you will be free indeed'" (John 8:33–34, 36).

What is sin? Essentially, it's trespassing a boundary set by God. Behind the action is an attitude that says, "Nuts to boundaries. I need to be free." And, at first, living without boundaries feels like freedom. But when a sinful choice becomes a sinful habit, and that habit becomes an addiction, you begin to understand why Jesus describes sin as slavery. Strange as this sounds in our day, Jesus taught that true freedom is found, not by those who do their own thing, but by those who do his thing.

Some time ago I was part of a foursome in a charity golf tournament. We used a "scramble" format, which means that only the best shot of the four players counts. All four players take their second shot from the spot of the best drive, and so on. Of my one hundred or so swings on the eighteen holes, only one counted—a long putt that went in by sheer luck. The rest of the day was not much fun for me.

After the tournament, another member of my foursome put his hand on my shoulder and said, "Greg, don't take this the wrong way, but I'd like to give you a gift. I want to buy you a week of golf school."

I was thrilled. Certainly a pro could help me up my game. I showed up at the golf school, expecting to join a class of a dozen or so others. As it turned out, I was the only student that week. The golf pro's only job was to fix my swing.

He failed miserably. It wasn't that he was giving me bad advice; I just wasn't taking it. My body refused to follow his instructions. It insisted on doing what came naturally, and consequently the ball rarely went either straight or far. That week felt like a prison sentence—five days of hard labor on a driving range.

On the last day, we played an actual nine-hole round of golf. Just the pro and me. He had a wonderful time. I did not. While he was hitting long drives down the middle of the fairway, I was in the weeds, searching for lost balls.

He enjoyed the freedom of playing golf as it was meant to be played. I suffered the consequences of playing it my way, unbound by the constraints of successful golfing techniques.

Is obedience to Jesus restrictive? Yes, but delightfully so. His purpose in calling us to live within the confines of his commands is so that we might enjoy life as it was meant to be lived.

I learned how freeing obedience can be late one night in the inner city. It happened after I taught a group of collegians Matthew 25:40, in which Jesus says, "Whatever you did for one of the least of these brothers of mine, you did for me." After the Bible study, I took the group downtown, to an area where many homeless people congregate. It was a cold winter evening, and I challenged the collegians to invite a homeless person to share a hot meal with them in one of the nearby restaurants.

At one point two students and I approached a filthy and foul-mouthed older woman who was sitting on a bench. She declined our invitation to join us for dinner, so we began to talk to her about the love of Jesus. That set her off. She launched into a vicious tirade against Christians. "You people talk about love, but why don't you have anybody who is home-less living in your home with you? Would you do that? *Would you?*"

We were speechless. But I knew Jesus was using that woman to speak to me. He had just told me that the way I treated her was the way I treated him. I couldn't stomach the thought of having her stay in my home, but I knew I had to ask her. *No way—I can't do it,* I thought. *But I have to. No, no, I can't.* Back and forth I went, and finally I said something that went against everything I was feeling. "Uh, would you, uh, like to come and, uh, stay with my family?"

Immediately her body sagged, and she grew quiet. "No," she mumbled. "I'll be fine here."

I'm ashamed to admit this, but I prayed a silent prayer at that point: "Oh, thank you, Jesus!"—because I didn't really want her to stay with me.

That encounter haunted me for the rest of the evening. *What more could we have done?* I wondered. Then it hit me: *We could get her a hotel room.*

So I went in search of that woman again. I finally found her sitting on another bench, wrapped up in what looked to be a brand-new blanket. I asked her if we could put her up in a hotel room, and she again declined. She looked content and warm in that blanket. It was all the shelter she needed for the night.

It wasn't until we returned home that I discovered the blanket that woman was wrapped in had been given to her by the two college students who had been with me earlier in the evening. After we left her, they went into a nearby upscale department store, pooled their dinner money, and purchased the blanket.

Not just for the old woman but for Jesus.

Was it a sacrifice for them? Did they complain that they had to skip dinner? No, they were pulsating with the joy that comes from living a life of freedom—the freedom of obedience.

Certainty instead of doubt. Freedom instead of bondage. If you want to know why it's worth it to obey the most counterintuitive commands of Jesus, start there.

Just don't stop there—because there's one more benefit of taking the leap of faith. We'll discover it in chapter 3, and I think you'll agree that it's the most valuable one of all.

# 3

## Minimum Requirement

IS DISCIPLESHIP AN OPTIONAL EXTRA?

His first name is Adam. I can't tell you his last name because then he might have to kill me. He could. He is a member of the Army's 160th Special Operations Aviation Regiment. If you don't know what that is, that's okay. Neither did his mother when he was trying to explain to her what unit he wanted to join. "They're called the Night Stalkers, Mom," Adam told her. When she still looked confused, he mentioned the movie *Black Hawk Down*, and that's when she realized that her son was pursuing one of the most difficult and dangerous assignments in the United States Army.

It frightened her, but it didn't surprise her, because she couldn't remember a time in Adam's life when he had ever settled for anything safe or ordinary. A quest for adventure and excellence was in his blood.

To become a Night Stalker, first you have to survive Green Platoon, a high-intensity five-week "school" that has more dropouts than graduates. Just being accepted into the Green Platoon training is an accomplishment. In fact, Adam failed in his first attempt. After weeks of getting "smoked" (think *cramps* and *vomiting*, and you'll get the picture), he was told that he did not qualify for Green Platoon. It was the most depressing day of his life, because if there was anything he couldn't bear, it was the thought of being part of what he called the "regular Army."

Then he was offered a second chance. And he made the most of it. It was just ten weeks later that Adam finished first in his class of forty. Although he had the lowest rank, he earned the highest score.

Since joining the 160th, Adam has endured even more rigorous training and has completed several missions in Iraq. "I guess my job is fairly dangerous," he said—but, for him that's a plus. And he believes that promoting freedom and fighting evil are goals worthy of full devotion.

I suspect that some who enlist in the United States Armed Forces do it for different reasons than Adam did. Some might even do it primarily because they like the benefit package. On the day Adam said, "Give me the toughest job you've got," it's likely that another young man walked into a military recruiter's office and said, "I hear you guys offer a free college education."

The church is no different. There are "maximum commitment" Christians and "minimum requirement" Christians. A man stares into the distance and announces to his friend, "I don't care what it costs me, I want to be a wholehearted follower of Jesus Christ." His buddy leans back in his chair and says, "I'll be happy if I make it into heaven by the skin of my teeth."

Both have valid goals. One wants to know how to live in such a way that his Lord will one day say to him, "Well done, good and faithful servant" (Matt. 25:21). The other just wants to be sure Jesus never says to him, "I never knew you. Away from me, you evildoer!" (Matt. 7:23).

## Faith and Discipleship

Which type of person was Jesus addressing in John 8, when he said to the Jews who had believed him, "If you hold to my teaching, you are really my disciples"?

At first glance, it appears to be a "maximum commitment" verse, doesn't it? Jesus is talking to Jews who had "believed" him. They had fulfilled what he repeatedly said was the minimum requirement for entrance into heaven. "For God so loved the world that he gave his one and only Son, that whoever *believes* in him shall not perish but have eternal life" (John 3:16). "Whoever *believes* in the Son has eternal life" (John 3:36). "Very truly I tell you, whoever *believes* has eternal life" (John 6:47 TNIV). Now Jesus is telling *believers* how to be all they can be—the few, the proud, the *disciples*. God's special forces.

At least that's how this verse is often taught—as the way to advance from the outer circle of Christianity to the inner circle of discipleship. Among those who believe in Jesus, we are told, there is a smaller group who earn the elite designation of "disciples." How do they do it? They do it by holding to the teachings of Jesus. Faith makes us Christians, but obedience makes us disciples.

It sounds right on. After all, didn't the apostle Paul say, so very clearly, "It is by grace you have been saved, through faith—and this not from yourselves, it is the gift of God—not by works, so that no one can boast"? Yes, he did (Eph. 2:8–9). So if we are not saved by works of obedience, they are by definition optional, right? Zealously pursued by "maximum commitment" disciples, but safely neglected by "minimum requirement" believers.

It's an attractive interpretation, and—if I may be so bold to say this—a popular one among many lethargic "Christians" who have no doubt that they are headed to heaven regardless of their commitment to obedience.

But what if not everyone who "believes" in Jesus *really* does?

## Unbelieving Faith

Watch Jesus spar with "the Jews who believed him" in John 8, and look for clues as to whether he considers them genuine Christians.

> **Jesus**: "If you hold to my teaching, you are really my disciples. Then you will know the truth, and the truth will set you free." (vv. 31–32)

> **"Believers"**: "We are Abraham's descendants and have never been slaves of anyone. How can you say that we shall be set free?" (v. 33)

> **Jesus**: "I tell you the truth, everyone who sins is a slave to sin. Now a slave has no permanent place in the family, but a son belongs to it forever. So if the Son sets you free, you will be free indeed. I know you are Abraham's descendants.

Yet you are ready to kill me, because you have no room for my word. I am telling you what I have seen in the Father's presence, and you do what you have heard from your father." (vv. 34–38)

**"Believers"**: "Abraham is our father." (v. 39)

**Jesus**: "If you were Abraham's children, then you would do the things Abraham did. As it is, you are determined to kill me, a man who has told you the truth that I heard from God. Abraham did not do such things. You are doing the things your own father does." (vv. 39–41)

**"Believers"**: "We are not illegitimate children. The only Father we have is God himself." (v. 41)

**Jesus**: "If God were your Father, you would love me, for I came from God and now am here. I have not come on my own; but he sent me. Why is my language not clear to you? Because you are unable to hear what I say. You belong to your father, the devil, and you want to carry out your father's desire. He was a murderer from the beginning, not holding to the truth, for there is no truth in him. When he lies, he speaks his native language, for he is a liar and the father of lies. Yet because I tell the truth, you do not believe me! Can any of you prove me guilty of sin? If I am telling the truth, why don't you believe me? He who belongs to God hears what God says. The reason you do not hear is that you do not belong to God." (vv. 42–47)

Are the "believers" to whom Jesus is speaking Christians or non-Christians? They're undeniably non-Christians! So what? So in John 8:31 he is not telling Christians how to become disciples; he is simply telling those who claim to believe in him how to know if they really do.

Did you know that the word "Christian" is only used three times in the entire New Testament? And the word "disciple"? It's used 366 times. The only passage that uses both words is Acts 11:26, which says, "The disciples were called Christians first at Antioch." If *believers* weren't called *Christians* until after the resurrection of Christ, what were they called during the ministry of Christ? They were called *disciples*.

And how do you know if you are one? You look at your "faith" to see if it bears the mark of authenticity: obedience.

## Saving Faith

We evangelicals are not accustomed to evaluating our faith by its fruit. We're afraid of doing anything that might dilute God's grace. We dare not link obedience with salvation lest we be damned for preaching a different gospel. But if it is a different gospel, which one needs to be corrected? John 8:31 isn't the only verse in which Jesus linked obedience with salvation. In fact, he did it again just twenty verses later.

> If you hold to my teaching, you are really my disciples. (John 8:31)

> If anyone keeps my word, he will never see death. (John 8:51)

Think this through. What's the difference between holding to Jesus's teaching and keeping his word? There is no difference. (In fact, "teaching" and "word" are translations of the same Greek term, *logos*.) In both passages, Jesus is talking about obedience.

If we meet that condition, what is true of us? We are his disciples (John 8:31), and we will never see death (John 8:51). It is only disciples who will never see death.

Now, don't get the order mixed up. Obedience does not save. It's faith alone that saves. But, as the Reformers said so memorably, the faith that saves is never alone.

What does it mean to believe in Jesus? It means to believe in who he was—the Son of God. It means to believe in what he did—he died for our sins and rose from the dead. And it means to believe in what he taught. If you say you believe in what he taught, but you do not follow his teachings, do you really believe? In college, I had a world religions professor who said something I've never been able to shake: "What you are is what you believe." That's precisely what Jesus taught.

So did the apostles. James said it this way: "Faith by itself, if it is not accompanied by action, is dead" (James 2:17). And John wrote: "We know that we have come to know [Christ] if we obey his commands" (1 John 2:3). Obedience *to* Jesus is the acid test of faith *in* Jesus.

Notice, I did not say that perfection is the test. Jesus, James, and John are all talking about the overall pattern and direction of our lives. They are not saying that true Christians never stumble. They are simply saying that, for genuine believers in Christ, obedience is the norm rather than the exception.[1]

## Obedient Faith

Understanding that will help you to make sense of all those passages in which Jesus links salvation with obedience rather than faith. Have they ever haunted you like they have me?

Not everyone who says to me, "Lord, Lord," will enter the kingdom of heaven, but only those who do the will of my Father who is in heaven. (Matthew 7:21 TNIV)

When the Son of Man comes in his glory, and all the angels with him, he will sit on his throne in heavenly glory. All the nations will be gathered before him, and he will separate the people one from another as a shepherd separates the sheep from the goats. He will put the sheep on his right and the goats on his left. . . .

Then he will say to those on his left, "Depart from me, you who are cursed, into the eternal fire prepared for the devil and his angels. For I was hungry and you gave me nothing to eat, I was thirsty and you gave me nothing to drink, I was a stranger and you did not invite me in, I needed clothes and you did not clothe me, I was sick and in prison and you did not look after me."

They . . . will answer, "Lord, when did we see you hungry or thirsty or a stranger or needing clothes or sick or in prison, and did not help you?"

He will reply, "I tell you the truth, whatever you did not do for one of the least of these, you did not do for me."

Then they will go away to eternal punishment, but the righteous to eternal life. (Matthew 25:31–33, 41–46)

A time is coming when all who are in their graves will hear his voice and come out—those who have done good will rise to live, and those who have done evil will rise to be condemned. (John 5:28–29)

Those are the kind of passages that make you avoid the Bible's red ink. But don't misinterpret what Jesus was saying. He was not teaching a different gospel; he was clarifying the true gospel. Salvation is by grace through faith, but the faith that is by grace manifests itself in obedience. We must never put the cart of obedience before the horse of faith, but neither should we put false confidence in a cartless horse.

The apostle Paul said, "Examine yourselves to see if your faith is genuine" (2 Cor. 13:5 NLT). But what do we look for, since faith is invisible? We look for that which is visible, our obedience to the teachings of Jesus.

And once we're sure we have met the minimum require-ment, we might as well pursue maximum commitment—because discipleship is not an optional extra to the Christian life. It is the Christian life.

# 4

# Love/Hate

## To Whom Will You Give Your Heart?

The best day of my life was the day I became a Christian. The second best day was the day I became a husband.

On that unforgettable day, God not only gave me the desire of my heart, which was to be united with my beautiful bride, Robin, but he also gave me that gift in the presence of the other people I love most in this world. My parents, my grandparents, my brother and his family, pastors and mentors, new and old friends—they were all there to witness our marriage and to share in the celebration that followed.

But something happened at the reception that created a dilemma. A minivan, graffitied with shaving cream and dragging aluminum cans, pulled up next to the reception hall. And my wife left all those people I love so much and got into the van.

I had a decision to make. Was I going to go with my bride or stay with my family and friends?

How long do you think it took me to decide?

I was out the door so fast I didn't even have time to say good-bye. Just a quick wave, and off we went. I never looked back.

It's not that I didn't love those I left behind, but my love for Robin was on a whole different level. When I was forced to choose between her and them, it was a no-brainer. My heart made that decision for me.

That's what happens when we have to choose between rival loves. We are loyal to the one we love the most. And that's why, if you do not love Jesus more than anyone else in the world, the day will come when you will turn your back on him to follow someone you love more.

The most determinative fork in the road of your life may not be at the point where you decide whether to *start* following Jesus, but at the point where you decide whether to *keep* following him when the person or people you love most in this world are going in a different direction. And at that juncture, you will follow your heart.

That's why Jesus said, in Luke 14:26, "If anyone comes to me and does not hate his father and mother, his wife and children, his brothers and sisters—yes, even his own life—he cannot be my disciple."

If those words do not knock the wind out of you, you're too familiar with them. How could Jesus—of all people—tell us to hate anybody? Isn't he the one who said, "Love your neighbor as yourself"? And even "Love your enemies"? How could he tell us to hate the very people we are commanded in other Scriptures to love? The Bible tells us to honor our parents (Eph. 6:2) and to love our spouse (Eph. 5:25) and our children (Titus 2:4). But Jesus says, "No, if you want to follow me, you have to hate them."

## How to Hate Those You Love

What does he mean by that? Part of the answer emerges when you track the word "hate" through the New Testament. Sometimes its meaning is not emotional but volitional. It describes choices we make, not sentiments we feel. For example, in Luke 16:13, Jesus said that if we have two masters, we will *hate* the one and love the other. His meaning is clear: We cannot serve one without turning our back on the other. And in John 12:25, Jesus said, "The man who loves his life will lose it, while the man who *hates* his life in this world will keep it for eternal life." Does he mean that we must deplore our earthly life? No, he means that we must choose loyalty to him over longevity of life. And then there is Romans 9:13, where the apostle Paul quotes an Old Testament passage in which God says, "Jacob I loved, but Esau I *hated*." Did God loathe Esau? No, but he chose Jacob. Sometimes, to hate a person simply means to choose someone else.

Every disciple of Jesus faces excruciating conflicts of interest. There are times when people we love object to something Jesus wants us to do, or somewhere he wants us to go. When we come to that impasse, we must side with him—even if it breaks our heart. He is jealous for our undivided loyalty.

If you think that sounds a little over the top, it may surprise you to learn that Jesus was actually toning down God's original expectation. Brace yourself.

If your very own brother, or your son or daughter, or the wife you love, or your closest friend secretly entices you, saying, "Let us go and worship other gods" (gods that neither you nor your fathers have known, gods of the peoples around you, whether near or far, from one end of the land to the other), do not yield to him or listen to him. Show him no pity. Do not spare him or shield him. You must certainly put him to death. Your hand must be the first in putting him to death, and then the hands of all the people. Stone him to death, because he tried to turn you away from the LORD your God. (Deuteronomy 13:6–10)

Be thankful that Jesus didn't say, "If anyone comes to me and does not put his loved ones to death, he cannot be my disciple." He doesn't want us to kill them, just to live as if they were dead. G. Campbell Morgan said, "If an hour strikes when there is a conflict between the call of the highest earthly love and the call of Christ; then there is only one thing to be done, and that is to trample across our own hearts, and go after Him, without any compromise or questionings."[1]

Harsh? Yes. But in order to be faithful to one person for as long as you both shall live, you have to forsake all others.

## What Makes Love Look Like Hate

The question is, what possesses a person to vow such exclusive loyalty? And the answer is simple: exceeding love.

That's why in Matthew 10:37—a verse that sounds very much like Luke 14:26—Jesus did not talk about who we must hate to follow him, but who we must love the most. "Anyone who loves his father or mother more than me is not worthy of me," he said to those whose highest earthly love is for their parents. And then to those who cannot imagine loving anyone more than their kids, he said, "Anyone who loves his son or daughter more than me is not worthy of me."

This is one of those verses that turns preachers into Greek scholars. "There are many different Greek words for love," we hear from the pulpit. *Agape* is the word the New Testament

48

uses, and it does not refer to how we *feel* about somebody but to how we *act* toward them. To love somebody with *agape* love means to do what is best for them regardless of our feelings. Matthew 10:37 is not a verse about our feelings. Jesus knows that we cannot help but feel stronger affection for our parents and children than we do for him, and he's fine with that as long as, when it comes to decision making, we side with him."

Okay, I confess: I have said that from the pulpit. But that was before I looked up Matthew 10:37 in my Greek New Testament—where I was shocked to discover that the word for "love" in Matthew 10:37 is not *agapao* but *phileo*. It's a word that could also be translated "affection" or "friendship." Unlike *agapao*, it is an emotional word. Jesus is not saying that we must choose him over those we feel the most affection for. He is saying that he must be the one we feel the most affection for.[2]

The apostle Paul says essentially the same thing in 1 Corinthians 16:22: "If anyone does not love [*phileo*] the Lord—a curse be on him."

Examine your heart. Do you feel more affection for Jesus than for your father and mother? Is Jesus a closer friend to you than your brothers and sisters? Do you love Jesus more than you love your husband or wife? Is Jesus more precious to you than your children are?

If not, what can you do to grow more in love with Jesus?

Ask any marriage expert, "How can I make my marriage affair-proof?" and you will get this advice: "Keep the romance alive." Why? Because when you fall out of love with your spouse, you are vulnerable to falling in love with someone else. But how do you keep romance alive? You work at it.

My dream was to take my wife to Paris for our tenth anniversary, but that turned out to be a little beyond my budget. So instead I planned a weekend getaway to the Hotel Parisi in a resort city near our home. And I made it as much like Paris as I could. I bought Robin several different cards, each with a different picture of the Eiffel Tower. I bought a CD of French music. I took her to the best French restaurant in town. I worked hard at romancing my wife that weekend, and guess what happened? I fell more in love with her than ever. Why? Because we did things that lovers do.

That same dynamic applies to your relationship with Jesus. If he is no longer your first love, could it be because you are no longer doing those things you did at first to stay close to him? What habits must you reform to fuel your affection for Jesus? You dare not be lax about it, because if your love for Jesus does not surpass your love for everyone else, you cannot be his disciple.

## Your Feet Follow Your Heart

Notice that Jesus did not say, "You *may not* be my disciple." He said, "You *cannot* be my disciple." That is, "You are *not able* to be my disciple." His warning is not, "Love me supremely or I will abandon you." His warning is, "Love me supremely or you will abandon me. The time will come when I will want you to go one way, and someone else you love wants you to go the other way. And you will go with the one you love the most. So unless, in comparison to your love for me, you hate your father and mother, your wife and children, your brothers and sisters—yes, even your own life—you are not able to be my disciple—because whoever you love more than me will steal you away from me."

For some people, the love/hate dilemma comes at the front end of discipleship. You know that if you follow Christ, you are going to disappoint or alienate someone else you love. And you have to make a choice. Two magnets are attracting you—Jesus on one side, someone else on the other. And whichever one has the strongest pull wins.

Jake and Mary are both from Jewish families. Both went through a process of seeking the truth about Jesus, and ultimately both concluded that he really was the Messiah. But then both of them had to count the cost of violating the expectations of their family. Jake couldn't help but follow Jesus, no matter what the cost. He was respectful toward his family, and he tried to help them see the truth he had discovered, but in the end he "hated" them. He chose Jesus despite his affection for them. And he is now living an adventurous life that will never end and that will only get better over time.

Mary made the opposite choice. I'll never forget the day she told me about it. Our previous conversations had been invigorating, as I watched her discover that Jesus is the way, the truth, and the life. She was standing right there at the fork in the road, and I just knew she was going to choose Jesus. But when I bumped into her in the coffee shop that day, I could see that something had changed. I asked her, "What did you decide?"

She said, "I decided I would rather be with my family in hell than to be without them in heaven." It was not a flippant statement. She counted the cost. And she followed her heart. She loved her family more than Jesus, which is to say, she "hated" him.

If the call to salvation doesn't bring you to a crossroads, the call to service will. You know that Jesus wants you to seek first his kingdom in some way that requires dramatic change.

Someone close says, "How could you do this to me?" That's when your love for Jesus is put to the test.

When my friend Kenny was a college student, he committed his life to missionary service. He began to pray over a world map, and the Spirit of God put on his heart the country of France. Kenny began to order his life around the goal of serving the Lord in France. But then he met the woman of his dreams. The longer they dated, the more certain he was that she was the one for him. He made plans to propose, but then she said something that made him hit the brakes: "I don't want to go to France." He had to decide: *Who do I love more? Him or her?* He decided to end their relationship. It was very painful, but in time his heart healed, and later he met and married a wonderful young woman who did want to go to France. Together they devoted a decade of their lives to building the kingdom of God in that dark country. Today Kenny is one of the most vibrant Christians I know, and one of the reasons why is because, when he came to his most excruciating fork in the trail, he "hated" a woman he loved because his heart would not let him forsake Jesus.

Jesus promised us that no one who leaves a potential spouse or parents or siblings or children for his sake will ever look back and say, "I got a raw deal." Loving him supremely is the secret to a life that is incomparably better than the life that we leave behind (Luke 18:29–30). But loving him requires "hating" some others along the way. Maybe you're standing at a fork in the road right now. You're caught between Jesus and someone else you love. And it's tearing you up—because you know you can't have it both ways. It's either/or, not both/and.

Really, it all comes down to a pretty basic question: Whom do you love more?

# 5

# Cross Walk

## WHAT DO YOU HAVE TO LOSE
## BY FOLLOWING JESUS?

Between April of 1967 and March of 1973, I pledged allegiance to the United States flag hundreds of times. So did Mike Christian. The difference was, I did it in an American classroom, and he did it in a Vietnamese prison cell.

Lieutenant Christian's A6A bomber was hit with anti-aircraft fire during a daylight mission in North Vietnam on April 24, 1967, and it burst into flames. He ejected safely, but he parachuted into an open field and was captured immediately by the North Vietnamese Army. For the next six years, he was a prisoner of war. For most of that time, he was kept in solitary confinement or in a small room with a few other prisoners, but then the NVA moved its POWs into larger cells, with up to forty men in each.

One day when Mike was permitted out of his cell to take a bucket shower, he found the remnants of an old handkerchief in a gutter. He snuck it back to his room and, for the next several days, cleaned it with tiny bits of bar soap. Then, night after night under a dim lightbulb in the corner of the cell, Mike transformed the handkerchief into a crude work of art. He ground up fragments of roof tile to make red dye. He drained blue ink from pens. He mixed the colors with glue he made out of wet rice, and smeared them onto the cloth. Then he filed a bamboo stick into a needle, stripped threads from his blanket, and sewed tiny scraps of material onto the handkerchief.

Finally one morning, Mike displayed his finished work to his cell mates. "Hey, gang, look over here," he whispered as he waved the cloth. The men stood and saluted the first American flag they had seen in years.

Every day after that, when the guards were out of earshot, Mike Christian hung his flag on the wall of the cell and led the soldiers in the Pledge of Allegiance.

One day the Vietnamese guards searched the cell and found Mike's flag. They confiscated it and dragged him to a torture cell, where they beat him unmercifully for several hours. When he was finally thrown back into his room, the other prisoners did their best to nurse Mike's severe wounds. Then they clustered on the concrete slab in the center of the room and tried to sleep. But not Mike. He located his bamboo needle and a few scraps of cloth, crawled under the light in the corner of the cell, and began fashioning another American flag.[1]

Pledging allegiance is one thing, but proving it is another. That's true of allegiance to a country, and it is also true of allegiance to Christ.

## The Cost of Allegiance

When I decided to follow Jesus, it never occurred to me that I was making a dangerous decision. I felt as safe pledging allegiance to him as I felt pledging allegiance to the flag. But there comes a day in the life of every disciple when we must add to our childlike faith a mature pledge of lifelong devotion to Jesus—with our eyes wide open to the potential cost of such allegiance.

That day came for the first followers of Jesus when he clarified the cost of discipleship in Luke 14. Up to that point in his ministry, throngs of impulse believers had pledged their allegiance to him. And why not? They had heard nothing but good news, and they had seen nothing but miracles. Their thought was, *Who wouldn't want to follow Jesus?* So how surreal it must have been when Jesus stopped in his tracks, turned to the crowd, and said, "If anyone comes to me and does not hate his father and mother, his wife and children, his brothers and sisters—yes, even his own life—he cannot be my disciple. And anyone who does not carry his cross and follow me cannot be my disciple" (Luke 14:26–27).

Go back and read the quote again. Especially that last line. It's bad enough that following Jesus requires hating those we love—but what's this about carrying a cross? Surely he doesn't mean that literally, does he?

Of course not, I've often been told. In almost every sermon I have heard about cross-carrying, I have been taught that what Jesus means is that I must die to myself. I must say *no* to my own desires and plans so that I can say *yes* to the will of God. In other words, the cross is a metaphor for self-denial.

I'm sorry, but I don't think Jesus was speaking metaphorically. I agree that he taught self-denial, but people don't die to themselves on crosses. They die. Physically. And I think Jesus is telling us that if we're not willing to die for him, we cannot follow him.

I realize that to say such a thing is to risk sounding irrelevant. Right now you may be tempted to skip to the next chapter because you're thinking that the odds are fairly good you'll never be crucified. But hear me out. There are a couple of reasons why I think Jesus is talking about real dying in Luke 14:27. First, I can't ignore the context. Look again at what he said in verse 26, right before he told us to carry our cross. He said that we must hate our own life. There's only one other place in the Bible where Jesus talked about hating our life. It's in John 12:25, right after he told his disciples that he was about to die. He said, "The man who loves his life will lose it, while the man who hates his life *in this world* will keep it for *eternal life*." The contrast in that verse is not between living for yourself and dying to yourself. It is between earthly life and eternal life. To hate your life means to lose your life in this world. That's what happens to people who carry crosses.

The second reason I can't help but interpret cross-carrying literally is because that's the way Jesus meant it the last time he talked about it. Don't miss this: Luke 14 is a rerun. Back in Luke 9:23, Jesus said to the twelve apostles what he later repeated to the crowd: "If anyone would come after me, he must deny himself and take up his cross daily and follow me."

There's self-denial in that verse, yes. But where does the self-denial lead? To the taking up of a cross, and to following Jesus. Following him where? Back up one verse and he'll tell you: "The Son of Man must suffer many things and be rejected by the elders, chief priests and teachers of the law, and he must be killed and on the third day be raised to life" (Luke 9:22).

Was Jesus saying that he was going to die to himself? No, he was saying that he was going to die. And it was in anticipation of his own *physical* death that Jesus said to his disciples, "If anyone would come after me, he must deny himself and take up his cross daily and follow me." Can you imagine the picture those words painted in the minds of the apostles? They had seen crucifixions before. Jesus was telling them, "That's what is going to happen to me—*and that is what you must be ready to let happen to you.*" Following Jesus means preparing to die—daily. Every day we must deny ourselves the expectation of comfort and safety, and we must courageously face whatever persecution our allegiance to Jesus stirs up, even to the point of death.

There's a scene in the 2001 movie *Pearl Harbor* in which an Army Air Corps officer asks American fighter pilots to volunteer for a top-secret retaliatory attack on Japan for the bombing of Pearl Harbor. He says to them, "The mission I'm asking you to volunteer for is exceptionally dangerous. Take a look at the man beside you. It's a good bet that over the next six weeks, you or he will be dead. Those who are brave enough to accept this, step forward."

That's pretty much what Jesus said in both Luke 9:23 and Luke 14:27: "If you're not brave enough to die, don't follow me."

## Cross-Carrying in a Tolerant Culture

We Westerners tend to step forward and pledge our allegiance without much soul-searching—because, honestly, when was the last time a Christian was martyred for their faith anywhere near where we live?

Granted, there are parts of today's world where it is very dangerous to be a disciple. I have a friend who took a mission trip to Albania. He was explaining the message of Jesus to a small cluster of people in a Muslim neighborhood when an angry bystander confronted him. "I want to ask you a question," he said. "Is Jesus the Son of God?" And then, before my friend could reply, he added, "Before you answer, I must tell you that I am a Muslim. And if you say that Jesus is the Son of God, me and my friends are going to beat you to death."

What would you do? Well, that's a hypothetical question, isn't it? Not for my friend[2] but for you, because you're not planning a trip to Albania—or to anywhere else in the world where it is less safe to be a Christian than ever before.[3]

But think about this: How safe was it to follow Jesus when he started telling people to carry their cross? How many of his followers had been martyred up to that point? Not one. Times were good. Christ's words must have seemed as strange to his disciples as they do to us. Little did they know that, one day, all but one of them would have to pay the ultimate price for their allegiance to Jesus. Thomas did not know that his body would be pierced with arrows by those who resented his faith. James and Matthew had no idea that they would die by the sword. Peter and Andrew and Philip and Bartholomew did not know that they would be crucified like Jesus was.[4]

Just because loyalty to Jesus hasn't cost you much yet doesn't mean it never will.

What Jesus did with those men on that day was to help them develop a habit that would prepare them for the ultimate test of faith. And years later, when they stared death in the face, their allegiance to Jesus was persecution-proof—because they had played that scenario out in their mind day after day after day for many years. They had carried their cross daily, and when the wood and nails were real, they were ready.

Jesus wants us to be ready, so that when it becomes more costly to follow him, we will choose courage over cowardice.

There's something else we need to realize—and this is what makes cross-carrying a daily sacrifice rather than a remote possibility. When Jesus said that we must remain loyal to him even in the face of death, he was presenting a worst-case scenario. He was not excluding the inevitability that we will be persecuted in less dramatic ways. Loyalty to Jesus might never cost you your life, but it may well cost you your job, or a relationship, or the respect of others. To carry your cross means to be okay with that.

Soon after I started following Jesus, I joined the Campus Crusade for Christ group that met on my college campus. They had a book table in the student union with a big banner behind it that said "Fishers of Men." I thought that was cool, until the day they asked me to man the table. That's when I had to decide, *Do I want to be that bold about my faith?* I counted the cost, and I decided that there was a low risk of being spotted by anybody who would think less of me because I was a Christian.

But, coincidentally, that was the day a co-worker I had known before I was a Christian showed up on campus. I hadn't told anyone at work about my faith, because I feared what they might think. But there was Tom, looking at me, and looking at that sign behind me, and looking back at me again. He said, "So, you're . . ."

I hung my head and said, "Yeah," as if I were confessing a sin.

Long pause. Then, suddenly, Tom pulled out a knife, held it to my throat, and said, "Deny Christ or die!"

Not really. All he did was nod his head and say, "Okay, well, see you later."

But I knew where he was going. Back to the office, where he was going to say to everyone, "Guess who has become a Jesus freak?" I died a little that day. I paid a tiny little price for my faith in the form of Tom's disapproval.

## Suffering for Jesus's Sake

In a great little book called *The Cost of Commitment*, John White wrote this:

> When Jesus tells you to take up your cross daily, he is not telling you to find some way to suffer daily. He is simply giving forewarning of what happens to the person who follows him. The phrase has no mystical significance. It is neither a call to seek suffering as an end in itself nor an invitation to undergo an inner experience of dying. True, you will "die" to your own ambitions, your own pathway in life if you resolve to follow Christ, but it is not to such a death that Jesus refers. "If you want to follow me," he is saying, "be prepared for what you will have to face. They put me on a cross—and they may do the same to you. They ridiculed me—they will ridicule you. You will do well, then, to arm yourself daily with a willingness to take whatever may come to you because of me."[5]

That's right on. To carry our cross means to maintain our allegiance to Jesus no matter what kind of opposition we face, and no matter how severe that opposition gets. We must never distance ourselves from him in order to save our skin, or preserve our safety, or even protect our reputation. Instead, we must die daily (1 Cor. 15:31), absorbing the inevitable persecution that comes to those who follow Jesus without apology.

Imagine going to the Vietnam War Memorial in Washington, DC, and seeing, among the 58,195 names etched in that black marble, your own. There are three men who have had that experience. Robert Bedker, Willard Craig, and Darrall Lausch were all incorrectly listed as killed in action, and their names are inscribed on that wall, even though they're still alive.[6]

Dead, yet alive. That's what we are. We carry our cross daily, ready and willing to pay any price, even the ultimate price, for the one who carried his cross for us.

# 6

# The Cost of Non-Discipleship

## How Dangerous Is It to Play It Safe?

I know *Braveheart* won the Oscar for Best Picture in 1995. I know it's a moving film about leadership and honor, bravery and sacrifice. But it's still one of my least favorite movies ever.

I mean, really. How can you stand to watch that ending? William Wallace, hero of Scotland and enemy of England, has been captured and is in a prison cell, waiting to be hanged, drawn, and quartered. He prays, "I am so afraid. Give me the strength to die well."

He is tied to a cart, kneeling with his arms stretched out on a short cross, and is wheeled through the jeering crowd that has gathered to witness his punishment. The executioner uncovers gruesome instruments of torture in front of Wallace, then turns to the crowd and says, "Now behold the awful price of treason." As the mob cheers, he turns back to Wallace and says, "You will fall to your knees now. Declare yourself the king's loyal subject. Beg his mercy, and you shall have it."

Wallace is silent. The executioner calls for a rope, and it is slipped over Wallace's head. "Stretch him!" the executioner shouts. Wallace is raised into the air by the rope. "That's it. Stretch him!"

Finally he is dropped onto the platform. "Pleasant, yes?" says the executioner. "Rise to your knees, kiss the royal emblem on my cloak, and you will feel no more."

Wallace rises to his knees, then to his feet. The executioner shouts, "Rack him!" Wallace is stretched in midair by ropes tied to his hands and feet. A horse pulls the rope taut, and farther.

"Enough?" the executioner says, but Wallace does not answer. He is dropped again, then secured to a cross-shaped table. His shirt is cut open with a hooked blade on a long handle. We do not see what is done to his body with the knife, but we can imagine it as we watch the agony on his face and the gasps of the crowd.

"It can all end right now," whispers the executioner. "Peace. Bliss. Just say it. Cry out, 'Mercy.'"

"Mercy!" the crowd shouts.

The executioner appeals to Wallace: "Cry out. Just say it. 'Mercy.'"

Wallace begins to speak. The executioner announces, "The prisoner wishes to say a word."

The crowd falls silent. Wallace raises his head and, with his last breath, shouts, "Freedom!" The axe drops, and we see his hand fall limp.

Next we hear a Scottish voice: "After the beheading, William Wallace's body was torn to pieces. His head was set on London Bridge, his arms and legs sent to the four corners of Britain as a warning."

This is why the DVD jacket says, "Rated R for brutal medieval warfare."

I suppose some are inspired by such scenes, but all I could think when I was watching it (and not watching it, at times) was, *That could happen to me.* I had studied what Jesus taught about cross-carrying, and I had decided that, yes, I was willing to pay the ultimate price for my faith, if it ever came down to that. But *Braveheart* gave me second thoughts. It made me count the cost at—pardon the expression—gut level.

## Why Carry a Cross?

Luke 9:23 is one of those verses that never seems to make it into gospel tracts. But when you visualize the potential implications of denying yourself and taking up your cross daily and following Jesus, you cannot help but ask the question, "Why would I want to do that?"

Here's the answer: Because no matter how high the cost of discipleship gets, the cost of non-discipleship is higher.

If you read what Jesus said about cross-carrying in Luke 9:23 without finishing the paragraph, you might miss the fact that, for every word about the cost of loyalty to him in that paragraph, there are three about the cost of disloyalty to him. Look at it on a ledger:

| Cost of Loyalty | Cost of Disloyalty |
|---|---|
| "If anyone would come after me, he must deny himself and take up his cross daily and follow me." (Luke 9:23) | "For whoever wants to save his life will lose it, but whoever loses his life for me will save it. What good is it for a man to gain the whole world, and yet lose or forfeit his very self? If anyone is ashamed of me and my words, the Son of Man will be ashamed of him when he comes in his glory and in the glory of the Father and of the holy angels." (Luke 9:24–26) |

Should we calculate what it will cost us to be all-weather disciples? Absolutely—but we should also compare it to the cost of being fair-weather disciples.

To help us with that cost comparison, Jesus said in verse 24, "For whoever wants to save his life will lose it, but whoever loses his life for me will save it." That may sound like a riddle, but Jesus solved it for us in another passage, John 12:25, where he said, "The man who loves his life will lose it, while the man who hates his life *in this world* will keep it *for eternal life*." Notice that life consists of two disproportionate parts: earthly life and eternal life.

Imagine if you could draw a line that starts where you are sitting and stretches all the way to the state border. No, farther—to the edge of the continent. Farther—beyond the curvature of the earth and into space. Imagine that the line goes on forever. That line represents eternity. How much space does your earthly life take up on that line? Hardly any. It's just a tiny little dot. Here's what Jesus is saying in Luke 9:24: "Whoever wants to save his dot will lose his line, but whoever loses his dot for me will save his line."

Of course, to us, earthly life doesn't feel like a dot. It's all we know, so it's natural to think only of the earthly pros and cons of following Jesus. But a short-term outlook can lead to long-term regret, so Jesus doesn't let up on us. He says in verse 25, "What good is it for a man to gain the whole world, and yet lose or forfeit his very self?" In the other Gospels, the word is not "self" but "soul." What good is it for you to gain the whole world, and yet forfeit your soul? If you could trade your eternal life for the most enjoyable earthly life anyone has ever lived, would you? Would it be worth it to have everything you always wanted for a few years before suffering for eternity in hell? Or is the better transaction to have your life on earth cut short, only to be welcomed into paradise for all eternity?

Jim Elliot was a missionary in Ecuador who was martyred for his faith in 1956. He was speared to death by members of the tribe that he was seeking to reach. But long before he died, he wrote this in his journal: "He is no fool who gives what he cannot keep to gain what he cannot lose." He had counted the cost, and made his choice.

## Being Ashamed

What will happen to you if you make the opposite choice? What if you distance yourself from Jesus in order to save your skin? He answered that question in Luke 9:26: "If anyone is ashamed of me and my words, the Son of Man will be ashamed of him when he comes in his glory and in the glory of the Father and of the holy angels."

The day is coming when Jesus will return to this earth, with unveiled glory and accompanying angels. On that day, every soul will reinhabit its earthly body, and all people from all of history will gather before Christ's throne. He will separate the people, one by one, into two groups—those who will inherit the kingdom of heaven, and those who will be banished to eternal punishment. You will be there, hoping to see a radiant smile on the face of Jesus as he welcomes you home. But imagine if, when you come to the front of the line, he looks away from you, silently, ashamed to acknowledge you as his own.

If you think that could never happen, look up Luke 12:8–9; 2 Timothy 2:12; and Revelation 3:5. (Go ahead. Put this book down, grab a Bible, and look the verses up.) The fact is, the cowardly will be among those who will be thrown in the fiery lake of burning sulfur. I didn't make that up. God himself said it in Revelation 21:8. We must overcome the temptation to be ashamed of Jesus when the cost of allegiance is high, because the cost of abandoning him is infinitely higher.

I'm not saying salvation can be forfeited through cowardice, just that it is proven by courage. The genuineness of our faith is not tested by how quickly we claim to be Christ's followers when times are good, but how resolutely we maintain our allegiance to him when opposition is fierce.


## Hope for Cowards

But this presents a problem—at least, for me it does—because I have had my moments of cowardice. And, come to think of it, so did those twelve men Jesus was talking to in Luke 9. When he was arrested, convicted, and executed, every last one of them was AWOL. And Jesus knew they would be. On the night he was betrayed by Judas, he said to the other eleven, "You will all fall away."

Simon Peter argued with Jesus. "Even if all the others fall away, I won't. I'll die before I disown you."

"Will you really lay down your life for me?" Jesus replied. "I tell you the truth, this very night, before the rooster crows, you will disown me three times."

Peter didn't believe it. But then he went and did it. When Jesus was arrested, Peter ran away. Then, when the mob marched Jesus to the home of the high priest, Peter followed— but at a safe distance. When Jesus entered the home, Peter made it as far as the courtyard. As he warmed his hands over the fire, he was recognized as a disciple. But he lied, not once, not twice, but three times, "I do not know *that man*." Not "Jesus." "That man."

After Peter's third denial, Luke 22:61 says that Jesus "turned and looked straight at Peter." Can you imagine what that must have felt like? After all Jesus had done for him? After he had been warned so clearly that he dare not be ashamed of Christ, lest Christ be ashamed of him? Luke says that Peter "went outside and wept bitterly."

But that's not the end of the story. After Jesus was raised from the dead, which apostle did he appear to first? Simon Peter. We don't know what he said, but whatever it was, Peter apparently still thought he was without hope and a future— because John 21 tells us that he went back to his old life, back from being an apostle to being a fisherman. Just like he had done right before Jesus first said to him, "Follow me," he spent the night casting his nets into the Sea of Galilee. And just like that night three years earlier, he caught nothing.

Early in the morning, he and the six former disciples who were with him heard a vaguely familiar voice from the shore. "Friends, haven't you any fish?"

"No," they replied to the shadowy figure silhouetted by the rising sun.

"Throw your net on the right side of the boat and you will find some." They did so, and they caught so many fish that they could not haul in the net.

For Peter, James, and John, it was déjà vu—a rerun of what had happened at that very same location three years earlier. John was the first to make the connection. "It is the Lord!" he shouted. And immediately Peter was in the water, swimming to shore.

When he climbed out of the lake, a fire was burning. There are different words in the Greek language for fire. The word in John 21:9 describes a particular kind of fire—a charcoal fire. There's only one other place in the Bible where that word is used. It's in John 18:18, the passage that describes the fire in the courtyard of the high priest where Peter warmed his hands while denying Christ. Hmm.

A meal was served, and Peter ate silently, staring at the glowing embers, rewinding and replaying the three denials.

Then Jesus spoke. "Simon son of John, do you truly love me more than these?" The word Jesus used for love was *agapao*, the self-sacrificial kind of love that he had displayed on the cross and that Peter had failed to display in the courtyard.

"Yes, Lord," he said, "you know that I . . ." And then there was a pause. The Lord did know how much Simon loved him—and it was not enough to lay down his life. So, with his head down, he said, "You know that I *phileo* you."[1] It's the word for love used in Matthew 10:37, where Jesus said that if we do not have a stronger affection for him than for anyone else, we are not worthy of him. Simon did love Jesus supremely, but he did not love him courageously.

Jesus had every right to disown Simon. But instead he replied, "Feed my lambs."

Again Jesus said, "Simon son of John, do you *agapao* me?"

He answered, "Yes, Lord, you know that I . . . *phileo* you."

Jesus said, "Take care of my sheep."

The third time he said to him, "Simon son of John, do you *phileo* me?"

Peter was hurt because Jesus asked him this third time, "Do you *phileo* me?" He said, "Lord, you know all things; you know that I *phileo* you."

Jesus said, "Feed my sheep."

How many times did Peter disown Jesus next to the first charcoal fire? Three. How many times did Jesus recommission Peter next to the second charcoal fire? Three. Once for each denial. Even after Peter did what Jesus told him he dare not do, the Lord gave him grace.

And then came Pentecost—the day Peter was filled with the Holy Spirit. From that day on, he never denied Christ. Not even when he was imprisoned and beaten. And not on the day he was crucified. Tradition says that he insisted on being crucified upside down, because he was unworthy of dying in the same manner as his Lord.[2] Ultimately, Peter did deny himself, and took up his cross, and followed Christ.

If you have ever been ashamed of Jesus, understand this: Your loyalty to him is determined not by isolated snapshots but by the whole DVD of your life. When you stand before him, he is not going to remind you of your most cowardly moments as a disciple. He is going to remember a life that either was or was not characterized by love for him—love that began as affection and, by the power of his Spirit, evolved into allegiance.

So don't despair because of your disloyalty to Jesus in the past. Just commit yourself to courageous loyalty in the future. Be brave in heart.

# 7

# Going for Broke

How Much Can a Christian Own?

The logo is so familiar that when it appears on a TV commercial, the company's name is nowhere to be seen. It's superfluous. You see the red and white concentric circles, and you know where to get what was advertised—down the street, at your local Target store.

What goes under the logo, in place of the store's name, is its slogan: "Expect more. Pay less." That's Target's appeal: better products at lower prices. There are some, I know, who are put off by discounts, but Target's popularity tells me they are in the minority. We commoners can't resist a good deal.

And what's true in retail is also true in religion. Some want salvation's price tag to be high enough that only people as righteous as them can afford it. But far more of us are bargain hunters. The more we can get for less, the better.

Maybe that's one reason why all but the arrogant flocked to Jesus. He offered so much more than his competition—a clean slate and escape from death. And he seemed to ask for so much less—nothing but repentance and faith. People who wanted more for less couldn't resist him.

You'd think Jesus would be thrilled. But he wasn't. He was troubled—because he knew something the impulse buyers didn't. He knew that the free gift of salvation leads to a costly life of discipleship. And so, not willing to pull a bait and switch, he turned to the crowd and said, among other repelling things, "Any of you who does not give up everything he has cannot be my disciple" (Luke 14:33).

How's that for an advertising pitch? *Expect more. Pay everything.*

## Looking for Loopholes

Read the verse in a more literal translation, and you'll see that "everything he has" means "all his own possessions." If that doesn't make you guard your wallet, it at least makes you look for loopholes.

Loopholes like: maybe it only applies to those who are wealthier than we are, or more obsessed with money. Sure, Jesus told the rich young ruler to give up everything he had, but he certainly doesn't expect that of every disciple—does he? Apparently so, because he was speaking, not to the rich young ruler, but to a socioeconomically diverse crowd when he said, "*Any of you* who does not give up everything he has cannot be my disciple" (Luke 14:33).

So we have to be willing to give up our possessions if Jesus tells us to? No, we have to actually do it, because he already told us to: "Any of you who does not *give up* everything he has cannot be my disciple." The word "willing" is not there, not even in the Greek.

"How about I give up *some* of my possessions?" Sorry. "Any of you who does not give up *everything he has* cannot be my disciple."

"On second thought," we say, "discipleship is pricey. I think I'll just take what's free. Salvation please, and hold the discipleship." That's like asking for a one-sided coin. Remember, when Jesus used the word "disciple," he meant what we mean when we use the word "Christian." (If you aren't convinced of that yet, go back and reread John 8:31–51. Check out Acts 11:26 while you're at it.) We can't interpret our way out of the conclusion that Jesus is saying in Luke 14:33 that part of what it means to be a Christian is the relinquishment of all of our possessions.

And we object, because that sounds heretical. I know that's a label you never want to put on something Jesus said, but how could he teach something so seemingly out of sync with the gospel of grace? Is it not faith alone that saves us? And is it not a free gift? Did Jesus not pay it all?

Yes to all of the above. But faith is not the finish line; it is the starting gate. The Savior we accepted is the Master we serve. And "no one can serve two masters" (Matt. 6:24). Do you know what two masters Jesus was talking about when he said that? One was God, and the other was Mammon. Wealth. If we are devoted to wealth, we will despise Jesus. Maybe not now, but the day will come when he asks us to do something costly, or to go somewhere quickly, or to stand with him resolutely, and we will look at him, look at all our stuff, look back at him, and say, "I'd love to, Lord, but I can't afford to."

If you own your possessions, they will own you. That's why now is the time to give them up.

## From Ownership to Stewardship

But that raises a question that if you want to be obedient but not foolish, you cannot help but ask: Does *giving up* mean *giving away*? Do we have to actually become penniless and possessionless in order to follow Jesus?

The answer is closer than you might think. It's just a page flip to the right from Luke 14. Luke 16 begins with these words: "Jesus told his disciples . . ." He told whom? Those who had met the conditions of discipleship. Those who, apparently, had given up everything. And what did he tell them? He told them how to "use worldly wealth" (Luke 16:9). To use it, you have to have it.

But you don't have to own it. And, if you are a disciple, you don't. Jesus does. Your money and possessions are now "someone else's property" (Luke 16:12). Whose? His. You gave it all to him when you became a Christian. And what did he do with it? He handed it back to you—not to spend on yourself, but to invest for him. You no longer have the right to do with it whatever you please; you have the responsibility to do with it whatever pleases him. Your job is to ask yourself, "What would Jesus do with all this stuff?" and then to do it.

That means so much more than holding everything with a loose grip. It means leveraging money and possessions to expand the kingdom of God.

Every Sunday at our church we give those who attend a program filled with inserts, most of which are ignored. But one week we included an insert that nobody ignored. It was a one-dollar bill. I explained to the congregation that each of them was being entrusted with one of several hundred dollars that had been donated to the church, and it was their job to be good stewards of it.

The following Sunday I heard dozens of stories about the creative ways our members used the money to love people in Jesus's name. But I didn't hear of a single person who spent the money on themselves. Why? Because they were keenly aware of the fact that it did not belong to them. They felt responsible to invest God's money in a way that was faithful to his priorities.

Of course, the reality is that God owns every dollar a disciple spends. That's why it's not enough to passively wait for his unmistakable promptings, and in the meantime hoard our possessions. He wants us to take the initiative to invest in his priorities now.

## What to Do with God's Stuff

But what are those priorities? If you want to be a good and faithful servant of Jesus, what should you do with the money and possessions he entrusts to you?

First, you should use them *to support his messengers*. Luke 8 tells of a group of women who accompanied Jesus and the apostles as they traveled from town to town proclaiming the good news, and it says that "these women were helping to support them out of their own means" (Luke 8:3). They were using their wealth to meet the material needs of those who had left everything behind to share the secret of eternal life. That's good stewardship.

A few months before I graduated from college, I was invited to become a short-term missionary to Eastern Europe. To take the trip, I had to raise financial support. I wrote letters to every Christian I knew. Some money trickled in, but as the deadline approached I was nowhere near my goal. I prayed fervently and expectantly. In fact, the night before the money was due, I put my phone next to my pillow so that I wouldn't miss a call from that rich last-minute donor. But the call never came, and I had to tell my team leader that I didn't have the money.

He said, "Yes, you do. We got a check from an anonymous donor, and it's enough to cover the difference. Get packed." So off I went, to share the message of Jesus with people behind the Iron Curtain.

I found it more difficult than I expected. The combination of my timidity and their apathy made me wonder if those who had supported me were getting their money's worth. But then I met a group of three friends—Helena, Jacqueline, and Erol—who all claimed to be atheists. Helena was the most spiritually hostile of the three. She wouldn't even talk to us about God. Jacqueline seemed more open, but it was hard to share our faith with her, because she was always with Helena.

Finally, on our last day of ministry, my teammate and I decided to invite Jacqueline, but not Helena, to have dinner with us. She accepted our invitation, but then later we learned that she had invited Helena to accompany her. So we started to pray, "Lord, don't let Helena come!" She cancelled—but then Erol invited himself. I was so dejected, because I knew he was as anti-Christian as Helena was.

But it was our last chance to share the good news with Jacqueline, so we went for it. And to my amazement, Erol did not argue with us but listened intently. And so did Jacqueline. And when it was over, Erol was asking for books to read, and Jacqueline was telling us, in broken English, that she understood what we were sharing and that she believed it.

Jacqueline was the only person I helped lead to Christ on that expensive mission trip. But in heaven, Jacqueline will track down my anonymous supporter and say to him or her, "Thank you for using money you could have spent on yourself to support Greg. I'm here because you did that." Let me ask you: Did that disciple make a good investment? How much is one soul worth?

The next time you get a letter in the mail from a missionary family with a request for financial assistance, remember that they are not the only ones who were called by Jesus to give up everything to go and make disciples. So were you. The only question is, is it your role to go or to give?

## Voluntary Redistribution

Another great way to be a good steward is to use Christ's money and possessions *to meet the needs of the underresourced*. In Luke 12:33, right after Jesus promised to meet all our material needs if we seek first his kingdom, he said, "Sell your possessions and give to the poor."

For a long time I thought that all God really cares about is whether people end up in heaven or hell. But two things opened my eyes to his concern for the underresourced: a concordance and the body of Christ. I looked up every verse in the Bible that contains the word "poor," and I watched Spirit-filled people do what those verses tell us to do.

It started right after Hurricane Katrina. Roger, a member of the church I was pastoring, felt compelled to drive to Louisiana and find a displaced family to bring back to California. His wife said, "Couldn't you just post something on the internet?" So that's what he did. He uploaded an announcement that read:

> WANTED: Hurricane Katrina evacuee family interested in a new start in Southern California. The family selected will be provided with employment, food, clothing, and shelter for a period of 90 days.

A family in Biloxi, Mississippi, answered the ad. As they drove west, another Christian family in our town donated their rental home. Home Bible study groups took responsibility for rooms. Appliances were donated. Kitchen cupboards were filled. Bedrooms were personalized. Patio furniture and a gas barbecue went in the backyard. It was our own little *Extreme Makeover: Home Edition.* When the family of four arrived, there were clothes for the kids and grocery cards on the counter. For a full year, not just ninety days, that family's needs were met by a bunch of disciples who for the life of them can't remember what sacrifices they made, but will never forget the joy they felt.

Now, the church oozes compassion. People bring bags full of groceries to church to give away. Families spend Sunday afternoons at the park, sharing meals with the homeless. Houses are being built in Mexico, orphanages repaired in India. Medical teams travel with mission teams. Hundreds of orphans are being sponsored. And all of it costs money that disciples of Jesus are gladly investing in people who are especially close to God's heart.

## Open Hands, Open Hearts

One more way that you can invest Jesus's stuff well is by leveraging it *to create spiritual receptivity.* "I tell you," Jesus said in Luke 16:9, "use worldly wealth to gain friends for yourselves, so that when it is gone, you will be welcomed into eternal dwellings."

What did he mean by that? Just that, when we are open-handed, it makes others open-hearted. If we are generous toward non-Christians, some of them will become Christians, and when we get to heaven they will invite us into their mansions and say to us, "I had no interest in your message until I saw what you did with your money. I am eternally grateful that you gave to me what you could have kept for yourself. It was your love that opened my heart to God's love."

Can you imagine that? That's what can happen when you invite neighbors over for a barbecue and serve steak instead of hamburgers. When you buy a non-Christian co-worker a nicer Bible than you have. When you subscribe to a magazine you don't plan to read to help a kid win a contest. When you pay the electric bill for a friend who is out of work. When you invite a co-worker to a ball game and pay for everything. You can do it in a thousand creative ways. Every time you use what God has entrusted to you to show generosity to those who do not yet follow Jesus, you are being his good and faithful servant.

One of the most vibrant churches I know of meets in a hundred-year-old building on the corner of 3rd and C streets in Julian, California, a mountain town of three thousand. The structure used to be owned by a Baptist church that split so many times that it shrank to nine voting members. When the nine voted on whether to disband, the vote was 4–4, with one abstention. Finally the one who abstained decided to vote for disbanding, and the church folded.

Its assets were given to a large church in a nearby city, and the leaders of that church asked a grocery store manager by the name of Rick Hill if he wanted to be a pastor in Julian.

On October 23, 2003, he was handed the keys. His plan was to wait six months before opening the doors of the church.

Three days later, a fire swept through the town, and one third of the homes in Julian burned to the ground.

Rick immediately put together an emergency response team. He drove thirty miles up the mountain, six days a week, and worked fourteen-hour days offering fire victims whatever was needed. The team he built fed displaced families three meals a day for a month. They helped families sift through ashes to recover what was left of their possessions. They set up a relief center in the parking lot of the nearby Catholic church, and they gave people whatever they needed. They helped rebuild several homes.

Nobody knew that the relief team was also a church-planting team until heavy rains came a few weeks after the fire. The team gave away ten thousand sand bags with "Hillside Community Church" stamped on the side. It was their one and only marketing campaign.

Rick decided to move Hillside's launch date up to January 4, 2004. That first Sunday, fifty-seven people showed up. Many of them had never been in church before. Since then the church has more than doubled in size. Today about 140 people who live in Julian attend Hillside Community Church every Sunday. That's 4 percent of the city. If 4 percent of the people who live in your city were to attend your church, how big would it be?

What has it cost Rick Hill to be a disciple of Jesus? More than most people are willing to pay. And how much joy does Rick exude? More than most people I know.

A poster advertising the film *Mr. Destiny* reads, "Would you give up everything you had for everything you always wanted?" That's the trade Jesus invites you to make in Luke 14:33. You can expect more, but only if you pay everything.

# 8

## Credibility Gap

### HOW ARE SKEPTICS CONVINCED?

Ignatz Semmelweis could have saved so many lives, if only people had listened.

It was 1847, and Dr. Semmelweis was the assistant director of one of the two maternity wards at the General Hospital in Vienna, Austria. His ward was staffed by medical doctors; the other, by midwives. Strangely, the death rate of women after childbirth was ten times higher in the doctors' ward. Some months as many as 30 percent of the women whose babies were delivered by doctors died of what was commonly called "childbed fever."

There were various theories as to why it happened, but nobody suspected it had anything to do with the fact that the doctors performed autopsies while they were waiting to deliver babies and did not wash their hands between procedures.

Then one of the physicians cut his hand while performing an autopsy and died after displaying childbed feverlike symptoms. Dr. Semmelweis connected the dots and hypothesized that contact with dead bodies could make living people sick. For the first time he ordered doctors in the maternity ward to wash their hands before treating each patient.

The results were dramatic. The month before hand-washing started, the mortality rate of mothers in that ward was 18 percent. The month after, it was 2 percent—and the month after that, 1 percent.

You would think that the medical community would hail Dr. Semmelweis as a hero, but the opposite happened. They dismissed him as a quack. In fact, he was fired from his position at Vienna General Hospital, after which doctors stopped washing their hands and the death rate of women went back up to where it had been before, and even higher—at one point, to 35 percent.

In 1861 Dr. Semmelweis wrote a book on childbed fever and sent copies to leading obstetricians in Germany, France, and England, but it received unfavorable reviews and was largely ignored by the medical community. He never did gain a hearing, and in 1865 he suffered a nervous breakdown and was committed to an insane asylum, where he died two weeks later at the age of forty-seven.[1]

What a waste. How could someone possess such valuable information, and yet have so little credibility?

One of the hurdles Dr. Semmelweis was unable to overcome was conventional wisdom. What he discovered was so far off the radar of other experts that the question of whether it worked wasn't even asked. It was so obviously unscientific that no intelligent person took it seriously.

But there was something else that kept people from listening to Ignatz Semmelweis: his abrasive personality. He had a terrible bedside manner, even before he made his discovery—and when others rejected his findings, he attacked them publicly. He circulated open letters in which he called well-known and highly respected doctors irresponsible murderers. Over time his behavior become increasingly inappropriate and hostile. The reason many people didn't listen to him was simply because they didn't like him.

The moral of the story? Our influence on others is not just determined by the truth we possess but also by the traits we display. That's one of the reasons Jesus was so influential. When he talked, people listened—not just because of what he said but also because of who he was.

Think about the truth he shared. He said that dead people could come back to life. How could anybody who taught something so ludicrous be taken seriously? And yet people didn't ignore Jesus. They swarmed to him. He was so popular that the Pharisees said to each other, in John 12:19, "Look how the whole world has gone after him!"

There's no denying that part of what made Jesus unignorable was the power he displayed. Miracles—such as the actual raising of people from the dead—tend to enhance the credibility of teaching about eternal life. But something else gave Jesus high credibility: his character. It was his love that made people listen.

## Closing the Gap

Don't you wish you could influence others like Jesus did? You possess the same truth he did (the secret to immortality!), and if the people you rub shoulders with were to ask you to share it with them, you could do it. But how often does that happen? The tragic reality is that most people we hope to see in heaven have no interest in hearing from us how to get there. We have the cure, but we lack credibility.

How can we close the gap?

The original disciples knew how to do it, but they were wrong. Their plan? Stick with Jesus. As long as they hung out with him, they knew that apathy was unlikely. But imagine their dismay when Jesus said to them, "My children, I will be with you only a little longer. You will look for me, and just as I told the Jews, so I tell you now: Where I am going, you cannot come" (John 13:33).

They didn't hear anything he said after that. All they could think was, "If you leave, it's over." They had never considered the possibility that they might have to preach the good news of the kingdom without the visual aid of an actual king. All they knew how to do was to point to Jesus and say, "Have you ever seen such love? Have you ever seen such power? Believe in him, and you will have eternal life." Now what?

"Believe in Jesus, and you will have eternal life."

"Jesus? Didn't he get crucified?"

"Yes, but he was raised from the dead."

"So where is he?"

"In heaven."

"Right."

The apostles could foresee it. Eyes rolling, doors closing, souls dying. If they couldn't show people Jesus, alive and well, their gospel was going to sound like a fairy tale.

And if that was true in the first century, how much more true is it in the twenty-first century? The secret of eternal life that we long to share with others was disclosed by a man who hasn't been seen in nearly two thousand years. That's a hurdle.

But it's not one Jesus failed to anticipate. In fact, he revealed the solution right after he acknowledged the problem—which was too soon for the disciples. They were still reeling from the announcement of his departure when he told them the key to enduring credibility. "A new command I give you," he said. "Love one another."

Blank stares.

"As I have loved you, so you must love one another."

A cricket chirped.

"By this everyone will know that you are my disciples, if you love one another."

Finally Simon spoke. "Lord, where are you going?" (John 13:34–36 TNIV).

I think it's safe to say they were on a different wavelength. But Jesus used repetition to drill through their density. Twice more on that same evening, he hit the replay button.

> My command is this: Love each other as I have loved you. (John 15:12)

> This is my command: Love each other. (John 15:17)

Can you think of any other day in the life of Christ when he gave his disciples the same exact command five times within the span of an hour? And this wasn't just any day. It was the day before he died. Why, on that day, did he keep playing the same sound bite?

He did it to save lives. That's why he had come—to help as many people as possible live forever. Now he was leaving, and the only way dying people were going to hear the secret of eternal life was by listening to his followers. But would they? Yes, they would, if they saw in his disciples the same love they saw in him.

Jesus did not say, "By this everyone will know that you are my disciples, if you wear Christian T-shirts."

He did not say, "By this everyone will know that you are my disciples, if you can answer every question skeptics ask."

He did not say, "By this everyone will know that you are my disciples, if you master felt-need marketing."

He said, "By this everyone will know that you are my disciples, if you love one another." That doesn't mean that everyone will believe our message, just that they won't be able to ignore it. They won't be able to dismiss us as quacks, because our love will prove to their heart—despite the objections of their mind—that we are true representatives of Jesus. They will be compelled to listen because they will be confronted with love.

Let that sink in, because so much is at stake. When Christians love, people listen.

## Where Love Starts

But here's a curveball: It's not the people we want to listen that Jesus told us to love. Did you notice that? "A new command I give you," Jesus said. "Love one another." That doesn't mean "everybody." Remember the context. Jesus was talking to eleven guys, all disciples. By "one another" he meant "the other ten guys in this room."

As counterintuitive as this sounds, Jesus said that if we really want to impact outsiders, we must love insiders—not exclusively, but especially. He doesn't want us to be so intent on loving non-Christians that we fail to love Christians; he wants our love to radiate outward, saturating the church before it spreads to the world. The apostle Paul echoed Christ's strategy when he wrote, "Let us do good to all people, *especially to those who belong to the family of believers*" (Gal. 6:10). We're not supposed to love outsiders less, just to love insiders more.

Whether the disciples grasped that on the day Jesus said it, we don't know—after all, it really was a brand-new command—but we do know that when they, along with all who believed in Jesus, were filled with the Holy Spirit, the love he poured into their hearts spilled out all over one another. "All the believers were together and had everything in common," Acts 2 says. "Selling their possessions and goods, they gave to anyone as he had need. Every day they continued to meet together in the temple courts. They broke bread in their homes and ate together with glad and sincere hearts" (Acts 2:44–46). And what effect did their love for one another have on those who observed it? They "[enjoyed] the favor of all the people. And the Lord added to their number daily those who were being saved" (Acts 2:47). Why? Because what the Christians had, others wanted. That's the plan.

Some friends of mine lead an international students ministry in the San Diego area. Every Friday night, between fifty and one hundred college students from dozens of different countries come to their home. They all eat dinner together, and then they have a time of worship that includes a greeting time, just like many churches do. But what happens during that greeting time is unlike anything I have ever seen in a church. The love that spreads around that room during those few minutes is indescribably powerful.

Then they have a Bible study, followed by conversations that last late into the night. Some students go home, but others spend the night, sacking out on a couch or on the floor. Week after week non-Christians come, not because they agree with the teaching but because they are attracted to the love. And over time, the love they see and feel erodes their skepticism. They know that Jesus is alive, because how else can you explain that kind of love? I get newsletters from my friends every few months, and every time they write about students who have become Christians through their ministry. Every time. Their strategy is to reach outsiders by loving insiders. And it works.

## Infighting Undermines Outreach

For fourteen years I pastored a church that was committed to *helping people find and follow Jesus.* That was our mission statement. We were passionate about seeking and saving the lost, and for the first ten years we enjoyed both unity and fruitfulness. Then something changed. We began to argue with one another about how best to fulfill the Great Commission. Slowly, almost imperceptibly, two camps formed. And one day all that underground disunity erupted, and before we knew it we had a church split. Two groups, both equally committed to seeking and saving the lost, went their separate ways because they disagreed about how to do it.

It happened while we were studying the Gospel of John. It was right after the split that we came to John 13. The words of Jesus pierced me. "Love one another. Love one another. Love one another." I preached them in shame.

A few weeks later, we came to John 17. I taught my fractured congregation the prayer that Jesus prayed for us.

I pray . . . for those who will believe in me through their message, that all of them may be one, Father, just as you are in me and I am in you. May they also be in us so that the world may believe that you have sent me. I have given them the glory that you gave me, that they may be one as we are one: I in them and you in me. May they be brought to complete unity to let the world know that you sent me and have loved them even as you have loved me. (John 17:20–23)

How ironic that we divided because of different outreach strategies, and yet both strategies were rendered powerless by disunity. There is no better outreach strategy than unity. There is no better way to reach outsiders than to love insiders. Our two shrinking churches spent the next four years beating our heads against the brick wall of that truth while we waited to regain respect in our community.

The question is not whether we have the cure. We do. The question is, do we have the credibility? Without it, ears plug and people die. Just ask Ignatz Semmelweis.

# 9

## Down and Dirty

### WHAT DOES CHRISTLIKE LOVE LOOK LIKE?

I told you the truth in the last chapter. I just didn't tell you the whole truth.

I told you that non-disciples will know that we are Christ's disciples if we love co-disciples. That's true. Jesus said it in John 13:35: "By this everyone will know that you are my disciples, if you love one another" (TNIV).

But there's something else Jesus said that is to John 13:35 what a battery is to a flashlight. It's found in a five-word phrase just one verse earlier, in John 13:34, and if you remove it from the equation, you drain all the power out of love. But obey it, and God will use you like never before to turn skeptics into seekers: "*As I have loved you,* so you must love one another." It's not your ordinary, run-of-the-mill kind of love that turns heads and softens hearts. It's Christlike love. That's what Jesus told his disciples at the Last Supper. "If you want people to listen to you as they listened to me, love one another as I have loved you."

Of course, that statement triggers the question: *How has Jesus loved us?* And the answer comes to us instantly, in the form of a picture. What do we see? A man hanging on the cross, pierced and bleeding. "This is how we know what love is," John later wrote (1 John 3:16). "Jesus Christ laid down his life for us. And," he added, "we ought to lay down our lives for our brothers." To which we whisper, "Amen," confident that we will never have to actually do so.

The cross is inspirational, but unless we think deeply about how to translate the self-sacrifice of that scene into smaller, everyday acts of love that require something less than actually dying, it can be impractical.

If I can say this without sounding irreverent, we need a different picture. We need to see what the disciples saw when Jesus said to them, "As I have loved you, so you must love one another." Notice that he was pointing to the past, not to the future. He was not predicting what he was about to do for them, on that hill outside Jerusalem; he was reminding them of what he had just done for them, in that upper room. Skip back to the beginning of John 13, and you'll see it.

> It was just before the Passover Feast. Jesus knew that the time had come for him to leave this world and go to the Father. Having loved his own who were in the world, he now showed them the full extent of his love. (John 13:1)

Watch Jesus. He stands up from the table and walks toward a basin and towel by the door. Normally the basin would be full of muddy water and the towel soiled by the dirt of the guests' feet, washed by a kneeling servant. But there had been no servant, and no volunteers, so the basin is empty and the towel is clean.

Jesus takes off his robe, wraps the towel around his waist, and pours water into the basin. As the room falls silent, he approaches the nearest disciple, and kneels. He takes a foot in one hand and ladles out water with the other. Dirt becomes mud as he massages one foot, then the other. More water is applied. Fingers separate toes. Finally he takes off the towel and dries the semiclean feet.

He moves to the next man and repeats the process. And to the next.

The only sound in the room is the dripping water—until Peter, always the one to break the silence, speaks. There is no way he is going to let Jesus wash his feet. But, as usual, he loses the argument. Jesus does wash his feet, and then the feet of the remaining disciples. When he finishes, he dries his hands, puts his robe back on, and returns to his place at the table.

That's love. Christ crucified, yes—but also Christ on his hands and knees. We look up at the cross and say to Jesus, "I adore you." He points down to the basin and towel and says to us, "What I want is for you to imitate me." "You call me 'Teacher' and 'Lord,' and rightly so, for that is what I am. Now that I, your Lord and Teacher, have washed your feet, you also should wash one another's feet. I have set you an example that you should do as I have done for you" (John 13:13–15).

Some Christians take Jesus's words literally and conduct regular foot-washing ceremonies. Some do not. But whether you do or don't, I think you will agree that Jesus was talking about more than foot washing. He was commanding us to love our fellow disciples in a foot-washing sort of way. Love is an abstract—which is to say, comfortable—term, but foot washing makes it uncomfortably concrete.

## Humble Love

It tells us, first, that Christlike love is *humble*. You have to swallow your pride to bend down and wash mud from between the toes of those who have less status than you do. Line up John 13 with Luke 22, and you'll see what happened right before Jesus did it: The disciples argued about which of them was the greatest! The way Jesus settled their argument was by washing their feet. He was God, the apostle Paul tells us, but he did not consider equality with God something to be grasped. Instead he made himself nothing, taking the position of a slave (Phil. 2:6–7). And, Paul says, "your attitude should be the same as that of Christ Jesus" (Phil. 2:5). "Do nothing out of selfish ambition or vain conceit, but in humility consider others better than yourselves" (Phil. 2:3).

I saw this kind of love on a singles retreat several years ago. I was the pastor, and married, so I had one less reason for being there than the other campers did. One of those campers was Brett, who was just as interested in making intergender connections as every other guy there. But he was distracted by the presence of another young man, Jeff, who was in a wheelchair because of severe cerebral palsy. Jeff needed to be fed, because his fingers couldn't hold utensils. He needed to have the saliva wiped off his face to keep it from dripping on his lap. He needed help getting dressed and going to the bathroom. He needed someone to push his chair when the battery was drained. All weekend long, the person I saw serving Jeff was Brett. While other guys were getting dates, Brett was washing Jeff's feet. I don't remember anything the speaker said at that retreat, but I will never forget what Brett did. He taught me how to love.

## Gracious Love

You'll discover something else about Christlike love when you think about the men who were sitting around that table in the upper room. There was Judas, who was about to betray Jesus; Peter, who was about to disown him; and ten other friends who were about to abandon him. Jesus knew it all ahead of time. Yet he washed twelve pairs of feet. His love was *gracious*. He forgave them—which is hard enough to do, especially when the wounds come from a friend—but, more than that, he did good to them. William Barclay wrote, "The more people hurt him, the more Jesus loved them."[1]

Once when I was scheduled to speak at a men's retreat, I made an appointment with the pastor to discuss the passages of Scripture I was feeling led to teach. We talked over lunch at a café near his church. When I told him I wanted to teach on the foot-washing passage in John 13, he said, "Let me tell you a story."

Some time earlier a man in his church, Don,[2] had an affair with his business partner's daughter. It cost him his marriage, his job, his closest friendships, and his reputation at the church. For a long time he stayed away. Then one Sunday, he showed up at church. People reacted in different ways. Some embraced him, some greeted him awkwardly, some shunned him. But he kept coming, and eventually a few men welcomed him to their weekly Bible study, which was conducted over breakfast at the same café where my friend and I were sitting.

One day, as the men were sitting at a table with their Bibles open, in walked the mother of the woman with whom Don had committed adultery. She was carrying a basin, a pitcher, and a towel. She approached Don and quietly asked him for permission to wash his feet. And she proceeded to do so, right there on the café floor, while four grown men wept.

I met Don at the retreat. The first evening, after I spoke, he stood in front of his brothers and confessed his sin, asking for their forgiveness. The entire group surrounded him, smothering him with grace.

It all started with one deeply wounded mother, doing for Don what Jesus had done for her.

Think about those Christians who have hurt you. Do you serve them even though they have wounded you?

## Hands-On Love

There's another quality in Christ's washing of his disciples' feet that is easy to overlook. His love was *hands-on*. Here's a deep theological question: Why did Jesus wash the disciples' feet? Answer: Because they were dirty. He saw a need, and he took action. That's what love does. It acts.

I can't think about this characteristic of love without getting emotional, because memories flood my mind of the time when my wife, Robin, was undergoing treatment for cancer. Our church family loved us in so many practical ways that we could hardly absorb it all. They paid for a nanny. They did our yard work. They brought us meals every night for months. So many disposable plastic bowls piled up in our kitchen that we finally had to dispose of them.

One meal in particular stands out. It was Thanksgiving Day, and Robin was too weak to cook. There was a knock on our door, and two ladies walked in with a traditional feast—turkey, stuffing, potatoes, yams, pumpkin pie. Everything. Robin broke down and wept. I still get choked up every time I think about it.

"Let us not love with words or tongue," John said, "but with actions and in truth" (1 John 3:18). It's when we stop talking about love and start doing it that we look like Jesus, and the world takes notice.

Dr. Fred Craddock put it like this:

> We think giving our all to the Lord is like taking a $1,000 bill and laying it on the table. "Here's my life, Lord. I'm giving it all." But the reality for most of us is that he sends us to the bank and has us cash in the $1,000 for quarters. We go through life putting out 25 cents here and 50 cents there. Listen to the neighbor kid's troubles instead of saying, "Get lost." Go to a committee meeting. Give a cup of water to a shaky old man in a nursing home. Usually giving our life to Christ isn't glorious. It's done in all those little acts of love, 25 cents at a time. It would be easy to go out in a flash of glory; it's harder to live the Christian life little by little over the long haul.[3]

But that's how most of us are called to live it. Not by being nailed to a cross but by picking up a basin and towel. I could tell you a moving story about a man who ran into a burning high-rise to rescue his co-workers, or a soldier who wrapped his body around his buddy to shield him from bullets, or a nurse who exposed herself to a deadly contagion to care for the sick, but I would have to find it on the internet, because I don't know anybody like that. I don't know a single person whose love cost them their life. But in my mind I have a collage of real people whose love has cost them their pride, or their grudges, or their time. I see Jim and Paula, caring for his dying, ungrateful mother. I see Christie, slipping into the kitchen to do the dishes while everyone else enjoys dessert. I see Chip, riding his bike across town to repair the car of someone he barely knows. I see Richard, bumping into someone who had hurt him and greeting him warmly instead of giving him a cold stare. I see Bill, texting his friend every day to encourage him through a job loss.

These are not $1,000 sacrifices; they are the 25-cent acts of love that give us the credibility to tell the world about the one whose love led him first to a basin and a towel, and then to a cross.

# 10

# Be Fruitful and Multiply

### How Can You Help
### Populate Heaven?

My wife was great with child, and the days were accomplished that she should be delivered. But she didn't. She was two weeks overdue.

So it came to pass that the doctor scheduled a C-section. Our appointment was at 8:00 a.m. A nurse escorted us into a room and gave both of us sanitary clothes. Robin got a backless gown, and I got a stack of blue paper: blue paper pants, a blue paper shirt, blue paper booties, and a blue paper shower cap. They came in to get her while I was still trying to get the paper clothes on over my cloth clothes. I figured it was going to be a little while, so I took my time.

It couldn't have been more than three minutes later that a nurse burst in and said, "What are you doing in here? Aren't you the father? Come with me. Now!" She rushed me into an operating room, and there was this woman on the table, with her protruding belly cut open. Her head was behind a curtain. I looked over it. It was my wife! They sat me down in a chair next to her head, and by the time I got the lens cap off my camera, a baby was being lifted above the curtain. I kid you not, it was that fast. "Come in, sit down, here's your baby; it's a boy!" They wiped all the blood and fluid off of him and set him on Robin's chest, and just like that, I was a father.

Sean got about two minutes with his mom before they took him away. I went with him. And wherever they took him the rest of that day, I was there. I was there when they cleaned him. I was there when they put that cute little beanie on his round little head. I was there when they put him under the heat lamp. I was there when they brought him back to Robin. I let her hold him for a little while, and then I said, "My turn." And I held him for hours that day. In fact, I slept in the hospital that night, right next to my son. My son! A new life that I helped create!

If you are a parent, I'm sure you can relate to what I felt on that amazing day. You understand the mixture of wonder, pride, anxiety, protectiveness, and joy that a person feels when they help bring a new life into this world. Six times in Genesis God said, "Be fruitful and multiply," and when you do that—when you help create new life—you feel as if you have done what God made you to do.

## Bearing Fruit

It's not God's plan for every person to help create new *physical* life, but did you know that it is God's plan for every

Christian to help create new *spiritual* life? In fact, in John 15:8, Jesus said that creating new life is what marks us as his followers: "This is to my Father's glory, that you bear much fruit, *showing yourselves to be my disciples.*"

What kind of fruit was Jesus referring to? The longer you have been a Christian, the more likely you are to think you know—and the more likely you are to be wrong. When seasoned disciples read the word "fruit" in the Bible, their minds tend to jump immediately to Galatians 5:22–23, where the apostle Paul listed the fruit of the Spirit—love, joy, peace, patience, kindness, goodness, faithfulness, gentleness, and self-control. Those are the character qualities the Spirit of Jesus reproduces in our lives. So, when Jesus says that he wants his disciples to bear fruit, it's natural for us to think that he is saying he wants us to become more like him.

There's no doubt that he does want us to bear that kind of fruit—in fact, Christlikeness is God's ultimate purpose for our lives (Rom. 8:28–29)—but that's not the kind of fruit Jesus is talking about in John 15.

In the New Testament, just as in the Old Testament, the word "fruit" sometimes refers to *new life.* Paul, the same apostle who wrote about the fruit of the Spirit in his letter to the Galatians, used the word "fruit" in his letters to both the Romans and the Philippians to describe the *people* he wanted to impact through his ministry (Rom. 1:13; Phil. 1:22).

And get this: Every time in the Gospel of John that Jesus used the word "fruit," he was talking about new Christians. In chapter 4, after his conversation with the woman at the well, she went back into town and told everybody that she thought she might have just met the Messiah. A crowd of people streamed out of the town toward Jesus, and, when he saw them coming, he said to his disciples, "Do you not say, 'There are yet four months, and then comes the harvest'? Behold, I say to you, lift up your eyes and look on the fields, that they are white for harvest. Already he who reaps is receiving wages and is gathering *fruit* for life eternal" (John 4:35–36 NASB). What fruit? That cluster of people coming toward him!

And then in John 12:24, Jesus said, "Truly, truly, I say to you, unless a grain of wheat falls into the earth and dies, it remains alone; but if it dies, it bears much *fruit*" (NASB). What was he talking about? He was talking about what his death on the cross would accomplish. He didn't have to die. He could bypass the cross and go straight back to heaven. But if he did that, none of us would make it to heaven. It is his death that gives us eternal life. We are the fruit!

Even in the immediate context of John 15:8, Jesus gave us several clues about what kind of fruit he wants us to bear. It was just a few sentences later that he said to his disciples, "You did not choose me, but I chose you and appointed you to go and bear fruit—fruit that will last" (John 15:16). Let's break that statement down.

- He said, "I *appointed* you." That's commissioning terminology. Jesus was reminding his disciples that he had given them a mission to accomplish. Mark 3 tells us what that mission is. It says, "He appointed twelve—designating them apostles—that they might be with him and that he might send them out to preach" (Mark 3:14).

- Pay attention to Christ's emphasis on movement: "I appointed you *to go*." Where do you have to go to bear the fruit of the Spirit? Nowhere. But you have to go somewhere to bear the fruit Jesus was talking about.

104

Later, he would say, "*Go* and make disciples of all nations" (Matt. 28:19) and "*Go* into all the world and preach the good news to all creation" (Mark 16:15).

- And don't miss the fact that Jesus wanted his disciples to bear "fruit that will last." What did he mean by that? He meant people whose faith endures. He had talked about those who receive the word of God with joy, but when trouble or persecution comes, they quickly fall away. He had made it clear that only those who stand firm to the end will be saved. No wonder he said, "I want you to bear fruit that doesn't fall away. I want you to lead people to persevering faith."

All of the clues point to the conclusion that when Jesus used the word "fruit" in John 15, he was thinking primarily about *spiritual offspring*. He was not talking about what he wants to see *in* us but what he wants to do *through* us. He wants us to be fruitful and multiply.

I know, I'm belaboring the point. But can I tell you why? It's because I don't want you to miss out on the joy of helping to create new life. If you follow Jesus long enough without bearing any people-fruit, you tend to stop expecting God to use you like that. You think, "I'll never lead anybody to Christ." So when you hear Jesus say, "This to my Father's glory, that you bear much fruit, showing yourselves to be my disciples," your mind goes straight to the fruit of the Spirit.

## You Can Do It

But even if you have been spiritually infertile for so long that you have lost hope of ever bearing the fruit of new Christians, the truth is that you still have unlimited potential to do exactly that.

You may protest, "How can you say that? You don't know me."

What do you mean? That I don't know how ordinary you are, or how flawed, or how shy, or how inarticulate, or how (insert your most glaring liability here)? That's okay, I still say you can do it.

Why? Because the power doesn't come from you. It comes from Jesus.

What you need to understand about the fruit in John 15 is that it is part of a larger metaphor—a grapevine. Each part of the plant symbolizes different people. Jesus said, "I am the vine; you are the branches. If you remain in me and I in you, you will bear much fruit; apart from me you can do nothing" (John 15:5 TNIV).

Which part of the plant are you? Not the vine. That's Jesus. Not the fruit. Those are the people Jesus wants to add to his family. You are the branch. So what? So you are independently impotent. "Apart from me," Jesus said, "you can do nothing."

Want proof? Go find a grapevine and lop off a branch. Then say to it, in your most authoritative voice, "Branch, produce fruit!" Preach to that branch. Yell. Sweat. Try to make it feel guilty for not producing grapes. And when the barrenness of the branch exasperates you, throw it away and go back to the grapevine. Notice the juicy clusters of ripe grapes hanging on every branch—not one of which exerted any effort at all.

The lesson is clear: All you have to do to bear fruit is to stay connected to the vine. *Remain* in Jesus, the newer translations say. *Abide* in him, older versions say. If we were to use an electrical analogy instead of an agricultural one, we would say, "Stay plugged in to Jesus." The point is, we are not the creators of life-producing power; we are merely the conduits of it.

There are two promises in John 15:5. First, if you are not plugged in to Jesus, you *cannot* bear fruit. And second, if you are plugged in to Jesus, you *cannot help but* bear fruit. If you will only stay connected to him, his power will flow through you like sap through a branch, and you will bear spiritual offspring. And it will give you that hey-what-do-you-know-I-helped-create-a-new-life kind of joy that no other feeling in the world can compare to.

## Embracing Powerlessness

When I was a college student, I received excellent training on how to share my faith. I was taught how to approach a stranger, how to initiate a spiritual conversation, how to explain the good news, how to answer skeptics' questions, how to close the deal, everything. And I became fairly proficient at evangelism, if I do say so myself. I didn't actually lead anybody to Christ, but what can you do if they don't have ears to hear?

One day a Christian friend of mine, George, asked me if I wanted to go with him to share Christ with students studying on the campus lawn. He was physically handicapped, and he had a learning disability. My first thought was, "No, I don't want to go with you." But then I figured I might be able to teach him a thing or two, so I agreed.

We walked up to the first guy, and, before I could get my rehearsed opening line out, George said, "Hi! Do you know Jesus?"

I was mortified. I thought, "No, no, no, that's not how you do it." And throughout the time we were together, I watched him make one blunder after another. What I couldn't comprehend was why people were listening to him more intently than anyone had ever listened to me. Over time, I saw God do amazing things through George. And I finalized realized why: he knew his place. He wasn't trying to be the vine. He was content to be a branch.

George is one of hundreds of people I have known whom God has used to help others live forever. They're unique in so many ways, but they all have two things in common: 1) They're all ordinary, and 2) they all know it. They all marvel that God could use someone like them to do something as miraculous as creating new spiritual life.

That can be your story, if you will embrace your powerlessness and plug in to the one who loves to channel his power through the most ordinary of branches.

# 11

# Abiding for Dummies

## HOW DO YOU PLUG IN TO REAL POWER?

My son Sean and I were both looking at the same object—an Xbox 360 controller. And we were both exasperated, for different reasons. Him, because he just wanted me to play the game. Me, because I didn't know how.

How could I? The controller had no less than fourteen buttons. Six white ones, a silver one, three gray ones, and one each of blue, gold, red, and green. Actually, the three gray ones weren't buttons but miniature joysticks that could be moved in every direction. So, according to my calculations, there are twenty-three different things you can do with your fingers at any point during the game. And Sean was frustrated that I wasn't doing any of them.

"I can't," I said, "until I know what each button does."

"Well, it's obvious," he said. I stared at him blankly. Finally he said, "Let's just play, and you'll get the hang of it."

So we played. Madden NFL. And I never got the hang of it. First I tried to memorize what the most basic buttons did. But the time it took for me to (1) review what each button did, (2) choose the right one, and (3) press it was long enough for him to score a touchdown. Or two.

Finally I decided to stop thinking and just push all fourteen buttons randomly. After all, that seemed to be working for Sean. But things went from bad to worse, until Sean finally stopped the game, and, shaking his head in disgust, took the controller out of my hands. "Dad, you're hopeless," he said.

He no longer asks me to play video games with him.

But sometimes I watch. And what amazes me is that my son never reads the instructions to any game. He peels off the shrink-wrap, pops the disk in the console, and starts playing. He knows what every button does, instinctively.

Sean is the embodiment of a term that has been adapted to the digital age. He is a "native." He doesn't have to be taught how to play Xbox or send text messages or post a video on YouTube. Somehow he just knows.

Some people are spiritual natives. Ask them how to do something like abiding in Christ, and they'll look at you like my son looks at me when I ask him how to use an Xbox controller. Their eyes will say, condescendingly, *You mean you don't know?*

Years ago, I read John 15:5, where Jesus said, "He who abides in Me and I in him, he bears much fruit" (John 15:5 NASB), and I realized that, if I could figure out how to do that *abiding* thing, God would use me to help other people live forever. So I was hungry to learn. A friend who wanted to help handed me a cassette tape (if you're a digital native, you may need to ask one of us old geezers what that is) and said, "Listen to this."

I did. It was a recording of a talk on "Abiding in Christ." The speaker first exhorted the audience to do it, and then he anticipated the question "How?" I wrote down what he said.

> "How do you abide?" Want to abide!
>
> "Tell me how." I don't have to tell you how. Want to! That's all, just want to! If you want to abide with Christ, you'll find a way to do that.
>
> "How do you do that?" Any way you want. Stop asking how, will you? Just do it! Don't ask anybody and don't tell anybody. Just do it! Want to!
>
> My steps aren't your steps, and if the steps aren't in the Bible, then what gives me the right to say that my steps are better than your steps? It just says do it.

I felt like stepping on the tape when I heard that. Obviously he was a native. Abiding in Christ came so naturally to him that "How?" was an unnecessary question. But when I turned off my tape player and opened my Bible, I discovered that the speaker had not done his homework. It may be true that Jesus did not outline for us *steps* to abiding in him (after all, it's not a technique), but he did reveal specific *commitments* that we can make to stay plugged in to him. In fact, there are three of them right there in John 15.

## Stubborn Endurance

The first is embedded in the verb itself. The Greek word is *meno*. Trace it through the New Testament, and you'll see why different versions translate it differently. Sometimes it means to "abide," in the sense of dwelling somewhere—such as in your humble abode. That's the way Jesus used the word in John 6:56, where he said, "He who eats my flesh and drinks my blood *lives* in me, and I in him" (WEB). To eat the flesh and drink the blood of Jesus is a graphic way of describing faith. At the point that we internalize the sacrificial death of Christ, acknowledging that we need him, we are grafted into him. That is the point at which we begin to live in Christ, and his power begins to flow through us.

But just as often in the New Testament, *meno* means to "remain." It means to stay put, to stick around, to endure. That's the way Jesus meant it in John 15:16 when he told his disciples that he appointed them to go and bear "fruit that will last [*meno*]." He spoke repeatedly about the insufficiency of temporary faith; our faith must have perseverance. John, the disciple who recorded this teaching of Jesus, wrote later in his life: "See that what you have heard from the beginning *remains* in you. If it does, you also will *remain* in the Son and in the Father" (1 John 2:24). And if you remain in the Son and in the Father, you will bear fruit.

When the church I had poured ten years of my life into split, it didn't happen overnight. It was a slow-motion catastrophe, glacial in both pace and demolition. And during those long and lonely months, all I wanted was out. Out of the pastorate. Out of the church. And, yes, to be candid, sometimes out of the faith. I couldn't make any sense out of my suffering, or God's seeming indifference. But somehow, a moment-by-moment IV drip of imperceptible grace carried me through that dark valley. And I kept preaching, Sunday after Sunday, right through the Gospel of John. When we finished the book, I grieved the waste of teaching such an evangelistic book at such a fruitless time.

Four years later, I received a letter from a man I had never met. He thanked me for leading him to Christ through my preaching, and then he told me when it happened: "It was when you taught the Gospel of John." Tears pooled in my eyes when I read that. Even in the midst of disillusionment and despair, God used me to bear fruit, and all I did was to not quit.

Every disciple is at some point tempted to quit. But if you grit your teeth and remain in Christ until your faith finally becomes sight, you will look in the rearview mirror and see how he used you, over the course of your lifetime, to influence others spiritually in ways you were blind to in the midst of your darkest days.

## Utter Dependence

But it's not just tenacious endurance that keeps the life of Jesus flowing through us. Think about the picture Jesus painted in John 15:4–5:

> No branch can bear fruit by itself; it must remain in the vine. Neither can you bear fruit unless you remain in me. I am the vine; you are the branches. If you remain in me and I in you, you will bear much fruit; apart from me you can do nothing. (TNIV)

What kind of attitude was he trying to develop in us? Clearly, it's *dependence*. He was telling us that we have no power in and of ourselves to produce any kind of fruit, whether it's the fruit of godly character or the fruit of new Christians. And the more that realization makes us rely on him, the more his power will flow through us into the lives of others.

Some six hundred years before Jesus said it, Jeremiah said it:

> Cursed is the one who trusts in man,
>> who depends on flesh for his strength
>> and whose heart turns away from the LORD.
> He will be like a bush in the wastelands;
>> he will not see prosperity when it comes.
> He will dwell in the parched places of the desert,
>> in a salt land where no one lives.
> But blessed is the man who trusts in the LORD,
>> whose confidence is in him.
> He will be like a tree planted by the water
>> that sends out its roots by the stream.
> It does not fear when heat comes;
>> its leaves are always green.
> It has no worries in a year of drought
>> and never fails to bear fruit. (Jeremiah 17:5–8)

When I was a college pastor, I gave out a special award to students in whom I saw the power of the Lord at work. It was a rubber glow-in-the-dark dinosaur. And every time I presented the award, I explained that we are just like glow-in-the-dark toys in that we are independently powerless. In the same way that the dinosaur is only able to absorb light from the bulb, then transmit it for a short time before returning to the bulb for a fresh infusion, it is only a vital, constant relationship *with* Jesus that enables us to do anything good *for* Jesus.

When one of the students to whom I had given a dinosaur graduated, he gave me a special gift—an iron dinosaur statue, the same size and shape of the rubber dinosaur I had given him. He had painted it green and had secured it to a granite base. He gave it to me to thank me for what I had taught him. Ironically, though, the iron dinosaur lacked something the rubber dinosaur possessed—the ability to glow. Every time I see it now, I am reminded that what gives me power is not what I am made of but whom I am close to. Better to be a luminous rubber dinosaur than a lifeless iron one.

The writings of Andrew Murray have helped so many to discover the power of powerlessness. He stressed it repeatedly in his book *Abide in Christ*:

> The believer can do nothing of himself. . . . He must therefore cease entirely from his own doing, and wait for the working of God in him. . . . The great secret of abiding in Christ is the deep conviction that we are nothing, and He is everything.[1]

If you haven't learned that yet, just wait. You will. Over time every follower of Jesus learns, in one way or another, that, when we try to serve him in our own strength, we fail miserably. Conversely, the more fully we depend on him, the more fruitful we are. That is especially true when it comes to sharing our faith. If I were to graph my efforts at helping others live forever, there would be two lines on it: a success line, and a self-confidence line. And you would see a symmetrical pattern: the higher my self-confidence, the lower my success. And vice versa. Only when I have been weak have I been strong.

## Simple Obedience

There's one more commitment we can make that will release the power of Jesus through us into the lives of others. It's just a few verses down from John 15:5. Jesus said, "If you obey my commands, you will remain in my love" (John 15:10).

So much for the mystical approach to abiding in Christ. Jesus made it oh-so-practical. If we want to experience his love personally and channel his love powerfully, *obedience* is required. In 1 John 3:24, John restated the same truth: "Those who obey [God's] commands live in him, and he in them." Faith connects us to the socket, but obedience is the switch that turns the power on.

Corrie Ten Boom, a Christian survivor of a Nazi concentration camp, experienced this when, after the war ended, she gave a talk in a German church about forgiveness. After she finished, a man who had been a guard at her camp approached her and told her he had become a Christian. "I know that God has forgiven me for the cruel things I did there," he said, "but I would like to hear it from your lips as well. Fraulein, will you forgive me?"

He held out his hand, but she could not lift hers—until she ignored her emotions and summoned her will. "Jesus, help me!" she prayed. "I can lift my hand. I can do that much."

And when she did, "an incredible thing took place. The current started in my shoulder, raced down my arm, sprang into our joined hands. And then this healing warmth seemed to flood my whole being, bringing tears to my eyes. 'I forgive you, brother!' I cried. 'With all my heart!'"[2]

God's power is released by our obedience.

So if we want evangelistic power—if we want to be used by Jesus to help others live forever—which of his commands would you guess is most important for us to obey?

I would go with, "Preach the good news to all creation" (Mark 16:15).

And I would be wrong. Jesus said that the single most important command we must obey if we want to bear fruit is this one: "Love each other as I have loved you" (John 15:12).

To whom was Jesus speaking? The eleven disciples. When? On the night the twelfth betrayed him. Was this the first time that evening he told them to love one another? No, it was the fourth. He gave them the same command three times in the upper room. Was this the last time he said it? No, he said it one more time just a few verses later: "This is my command: Love each other" (John 15:17). And what did Jesus say will happen if we obey that command? All people will know that we are his disciples (John 13:35), and we will bear fruit (John 15:5).

Forgive me for repeating myself, but Jesus did: The best way to create new Christians is by loving existing Christians. Every time we love one another, the power of Jesus flows through us into the life of every non-Christian who is watching. They see our love, and it makes them want his love.

Several years ago I went to a Christian retreat that was attended by about two hundred people. Toward the end of the weekend a young woman committed her life to Christ. One of her friends asked her what it was that drew her to him, and she didn't talk about anything she heard, only what she saw: "I've never seen 200 people love each other so much."

Maybe you thought God only uses evangelism natives to help others live forever. No, he pours his life-giving power through every Christian who is committed to stubborn endurance, utter dependence, and simple obedience. That's how to abide in Christ, and that's how to bear much fruit.

# 12

# Search and Rescue

## DO YOU HAVE TO GO OUT?

The state of Massachusetts has straight borders on three sides, but its eastern edge spills out into the Atlantic and splatters it with all sizes and shapes of peninsulas and islands. The southernmost island in the state is Nantucket, and in the harbor of that island there is a tiny museum called the Nantucket Life-Saving Museum. It memorializes a volunteer organization that was formed in 1785—the Massachusetts Humane Society.

But they didn't save pets; they saved people. Nantucket was nicknamed "The Graveyard of the Atlantic" because of the ocean storms that produced violent waves in the shallow water surrounding the island. More than seven hundred shipwrecks have occurred off Nantucket, and a great many sailors have lost their lives.

There was a group of islanders in the late 1700s who could not bear the thought of all those people dying so close to them. So they formed the Humane Society. All along the coastline they built little huts and stocked them with emergency supplies and lifesaving boats. They came to be known as "huts of refuge," and volunteers manned them twenty-four hours a day. When they saw a shipwreck, they called for help and headed into the water. They risked their lives to save as many people as they could. Those who made it to shore alive were welcomed into those huts of refuge, where dry firewood and blankets awaited them.

The motto of the Massachusetts Humane Society was "You have to go out, but you don't have to come back." How's that for a recruiting pitch? Hundreds of people signed on, and hundreds of people were saved—sometimes at the cost of rescuers' lives—because of the willingness of those islanders to take tremendous risks and make huge sacrifices to save people they didn't even know.

It wasn't until almost ninety years later, in 1871, that the U.S. Coast Guard began to pay people to do what those volunteers had done. For a time paid workers and volunteers worked side by side, but eventually the decision was made to just let the professionals do it. The volunteers decided they no longer had to go out.

But there was one thing that they did continue to do, and that was to meet together. The Life-Saving Association, as it had come to be called, became a social club, where those who had once come together to save lives could meet together to reminisce about their adventures.

Today, the old Life-Saving Association is called the U.S. Life-Saving Heritage Association. And you can join it, for a small annual fee. With your membership you will get a quarterly magazine called *Wreck & Rescue*, a newsletter called *Life Lines*, and a 10 percent discount at a nearby bed-and-breakfast. According to the association's website, as a member you will read about the history of heroic rescues, meet the leading authors and historians in the field, enjoy the fellowship and intellectual stimulation of the annual conference, and help save the last of America's architecturally significant lifesaving and lifeboat stations.

I first heard about the Massachusetts Humane Society from John Ortberg, who visited the Nantucket Life-Saving Museum and saw in it a parallel to the church. He said:

> It doesn't happen in a day. It doesn't happen in a month. But over time, a church forgets it is in the life saving business. It usually doesn't disband, at least not until much later. People still meet. They still enjoy each other's company. They still use words like community. They still have services and buildings and staffs and programs. They might even be involved in various forms of community service. They are just not sending out teams any more for people who are going down. They are just not really scouring neighborhoods and offices, schools and networks and cities to see if there is somebody that needs to be saved.[1]

I don't know how those words hit you, but they make me just a tad defensive. I want to say to John, "Not every Christian has the gift of evangelism, you know. What's wrong with serving the Lord by helping to make my church a lighthouse rather than going out in a rescue raft? After all, Jesus said that we'll bear fruit if we abide in him, and we'll abide in him if we love one another. Isn't that enough?"

It's a fair question, and a priority-shaping one. Is it okay with Jesus if those of us who are not wired for outreach focus on in-reach? Or does he say to every single disciple, "You have to go out"? I don't think the answer is obvious, or else we would never argue about it. But I do think it is revealed to those who have eyes to see and ears to hear. So let's watch and listen.

## Jesus Went Out

And let's begin with the undeniable: Jesus was into outreach. He was a friend of sinners. When members of the clergy criticized him for the company he kept, he explained, "It is not the healthy who need a doctor, but the sick. I have not come to call the righteous, but sinners to repentance" (Luke 5:31–32). This answer did not satisfy the ministerial association. Their consensus was that a holy messiah would never hang out with unholy men and women.

They were still disparaging Jesus ten chapters later, and so he spoke to them in parables. Three in a row, all about the joy of recovering something of value. First, a sheep. What owner of 100 would not go out from among the safe ninety-nine to find the lost one—and, after finding it, throw a party? "I tell you that in the same way there will be more rejoicing in heaven over one sinner who repents than over ninety-nine righteous persons who do not need to repent" (Luke 15:7).

The saints were unmoved. So Jesus told them another story, this one about something he knew they could relate to—the joy of finding lost cash. "In the same way, I tell you, there is rejoicing in the presence of the angels of God over one sinner who repents" (Luke 15:10).

Their arms were still crossed. So Jesus told them a third story, a tear-jerker about a father and a son. Two sons, actually—one who was lost and found, the other who never left. When the returning prodigal got a welcome-home party, his squeaky-clean brother was as offended as those to whom Jesus was telling the story. And what the father said to his angry son, Jesus was saying to his angry critics. It wasn't a scolding so much as an expression of bewilderment. "My son . . . you are always with me, and everything I have is yours. But we had to celebrate and be glad, because this brother of yours was dead and is alive again; he was lost and is found" (Luke 15:31–32). How could God not be pre-occupied with the children he has lost? And how could his most joyous celebrations not be over those who are found? And how could it not be the mission of his one and only Son to go out and bring lost children back home? To Jesus, it was a no-brainer.

But were the religious leaders persuaded by the parables? No. Four chapters later, when Jesus invited himself to the home of Zacchaeus the tax collector, they hit the replay button. "He has gone to be the guest of a sinner." Tsk-tsk.

But after they ranted, Zacchaeus repented. And Jesus rejoiced. Then he explained, one last time, why he had to go out—from heaven to earth, and from the synagogue to the streets. "For the Son of Man came to seek and to save what was lost" (Luke 19:10).

That was the mission of Jesus. It was the highest priority and the consuming passion of his life. He was so committed to that calling, in fact, that he gave up his life for it. He made the ultimate sacrifice to rescue those who were going down.

## The Apostles Went Out

The second thing we can all agree on is that Jesus gave at least *some* of his disciples the same mission that had been given to him. What did he say to the two fishermen who became his first two disciples? "Come, follow me . . . and I will make you fishers of men" (Mark 1:17). Right from the start, they knew that following him meant rescuing others.

Later, Jesus chose from among all his disciples an inner circle of twelve, "designating them apostles" (Mark 3:14). That is, he gave them a team name: "Sent-out ones." Why? "That they might be with him and that he might send them out to preach." Sure enough, "they went out and preached that people should repent" (Mark 6:12).

On the night Jesus was betrayed by one of his apostles, he reminded the other eleven that he had appointed them to go out and lead others to enduring faith (John 15:16). When he prayed for them that night, he said to God the Father, "As you sent me into the world, I have sent them into the world" (John 17:18). In other words, "I have given them the mission you gave me"—which was what? To seek and to save what was lost.

And the first time Jesus appeared to the disciples after he rose from the dead, what did he say to them? First, "Peace be with you" (John 20:19, 21). He had to say it twice because they were a little freaked out. But as soon as they calmed down, he said what he had come to say: "As the Father has sent me, I am sending you" (John 20:21). He was telling them, "You have to go out."

And then there was the day he ascended to heaven. He knew that the words he spoke to the apostles would be his last in a long, long time. What they wanted to know before he left was when he was going to restore Israel's independence. But Jesus had something else on his mind. After he didn't answer their question, he said, "But you will receive power when the Holy Spirit comes on you; and you will be my witnesses in Jerusalem, and in all Judea and Samaria, and to the ends of the earth" (Acts 1:8). Then up he went. And out the disciples went, taking risks and making sacrifices to rescue people in peril.

## You Have to Go Out

But what biblical basis is there for the argument that all Christians should do what the apostles did? After all, there were more disciples than just the Twelve, but it was only those twelve that Jesus sent out to proclaim the gospel. Oh yeah—there was also that group of seventy-two others in Luke 10. And not only did Jesus send them out as his representatives; he also told them, "The harvest is plentiful, but the workers are few. Ask the Lord of the harvest, therefore, to send out workers into his harvest field" (Luke 10:2). Jesus knew that a great many more people could be rescued from death if only God would send more lifesavers out.

That should motivate us to pray that God will call more people into ministry. And if you have the gift of evangelism, it might even inspire you to answer that call. But if we're looking for a passage where Jesus teaches that all Christians should be as committed to seeking and saving the lost as he and the apostles were, this is not it.

Does such a passage even exist?

Yes. One.[2]

I'm not sure if you detected it, but in my summary of what Jesus taught about going out, I left out the Great Commission.

(Oh yeah, that.) Jesus said it sometime between the day he rose from the dead and the day he returned to heaven—and it is, to my knowledge, the only passage in the four Gospels that gives us no room to wiggle out of our lifesaving responsibility.

> All authority in heaven and on earth has been given to me. Therefore go and make disciples of all nations, baptizing them in the name of the Father and of the Son and of the Holy Spirit, and teaching them to obey everything I have commanded you. And surely I am with you always, to the very end of the age. (Matthew 28:18–20)

If you're looking for a loophole, you'll point out that Jesus did not give this commission to every Christian but to the eleven apostles. Yes, but what did Jesus tell them to do? He told them to teach others to obey everything he had commanded them.

Do you realize what that means? It means that everything Jesus told the apostles to do, he expects every disciple to do! If he commanded them to go out—to fish for people, to preach the kingdom of God, to bear fruit, to be his witnesses, to make disciples—then guess what? He commands you and me to do it too.

### Let the Pros Do It

Case closed? Not for the charter members of Jerusalem Community Church, founded on the day of Pentecost. Surely the apostles taught them the Great Commission, and they said, "Amen. We agree that you apostles are to go and make disciples, in Jerusalem, in all Judea and Samaria, and to the ends of the earth. And we will support you every step of the way."

So the apostles went out. Peter, the senior apostle whose Spirit-filled preaching in Acts 2 launched the church, continued to share the good news in chapter 3. In chapter 4, John added his voice to Peter's. So many people believed in Jesus that the anti-Jesus authorities threw them in jail. When the apostles were released, the church had a prayer meeting. With one voice they cried out to the Lord, "Enable your servants to speak your word with great boldness" (Acts 4:29). The servants they had in mind, of course, were the apostles. But what happened after they prayed? "They were *all* filled with the Holy Spirit and spoke the word of God boldly" (Acts 4:31). Hint, hint. But they didn't get it. As soon as they left the prayer meeting, the laypeople clammed up.

Meanwhile, "with great power *the apostles* continued to testify to the resurrection of the Lord Jesus" (Acts 4:33). In chapter 5, all eleven share their faith.

Then, in chapter 6, for the first time, one volunteer gets in the game. Stephen is the first non-apostle to "go and make disciples." And do you know what happened to him? He got stoned to death—a compelling argument for leaving evangelism to the professionals.

But you have to read what happened next. "On that day," Acts 8:1 says, "a great persecution broke out against the church at Jerusalem, and *all except the apostles* were scattered throughout Judea and Samaria."

Where did Jesus tell the apostles they would be his witnesses? In Jerusalem, and where else? In all Judea and Samaria! Who went there? All except the apostles. That presents a problem. Who's going to share the message if none of the professional evangelists are around?

It was at that point, I think, that the light went on inside the heads of those ordinary Christians—because Acts 8:4 says, "Those who had been scattered preached the word wherever they went."

Do you see God's plan? It's for every disciple of Jesus to seek and to save the lost. You have to go out, whether you do or do not have the gift of evangelism, whether you are an extrovert or an introvert, whether you are silver-tongued or tongue-tied, whether you have been following Jesus for decades or for days. Somehow, you have to find a way to share your faith in a way that fits your personality. And if you can't do that, you have to ignore your personality and do it anyway. Where you go, to whom you go, and how you go are questions that can have several right answers, but whether you should go has only one.

*Yes.*

# 13

# The Power of One

As a father of three, I have seen more animated films than live-action ones—including everything with *Shrek* in the title. In *Shrek the Third*, there is a scene in which Shrek, an expectant father, has a nightmare about babies. It begins with one needy infant crying uncontrollably. As Shrek tries to comfort him, a second baby crawls by. Then a third flies across the room, having been launched by a fourth from the recliner. Soon the house is full of babies, playing with knives and matches, splashing in a kettle of water, breaking glass jars, falling from shelves. As Shrek ricochets around the house saving each one, the windowpanes snap, and thousands more stampede into the house. Countless more cascade down the chimney. Finally Shrek is running in place from a tsunami of little green ogres.[1]

When he wakes up in a cold sweat, he realizes it was just a dream. But that cartoon comedy allegorizes the real-life tragedy that Jesus experienced. He poured his life into a black hole of human need. For every hurting person he helped, ten more showed up. The ratio of people who wanted a piece of him to those who got it grew, even as he exhausted himself serving as many as he could.

Imagine the emotional toll that must have taken on Jesus. He knew that those unmet physical needs represented a tiny fraction of the needs of the nation of Israel . . . and that Israel was just a speck on a globe malignant with suffering . . . and that, beyond the physical sickness that drove some to him, was a terminal spiritual disease that had infected every single person on the planet . . . and that the pandemic would mushroom with the population, killing billions over the next two millennia. He was willing to give up his life to provide a vaccine, but how could he get that vaccine to the ends of the earth, and to the twenty-first century, so that people like you and me might live rather than die?

Remarkably, he did it. Today, there are more than two billion professing Christians in the world. I'll admit the number is inexact. You have to subtract nominal Christians from the total. But you also have to add genuine Christians from every generation over the past twenty-one centuries. Whatever the actual number, I doubt you'll find a more successful rescue effort than the one launched by Jesus.

## How Jesus Did It

How did he pull it off? How was he able to give his full attention to one person at a time, and yet touch two billion?

He cloned himself. Very early in his ministry, after investing a night in prayer, "he appointed twelve—designating them apostles—that they might be with him and that he might send them out to preach and to have authority to drive out demons" (Mark 3:14–15). Rather than frantically trying to reach the world single-handedly, Jesus strategically invested some of his time and energy in reproducing his lifestyle in a small number of other people. That in itself multiplied his impact elevenfold.

But then he did something that made the growth curve go exponential: He told the eleven to do the same thing.

> All authority in heaven and on earth has been given to me. Therefore go and make disciples of all nations, baptizing them in the name of the Father and of the Son and of the Holy Spirit, and teaching them to obey everything I have commanded you. And surely I am with you always, to the very end of the age. (Matthew 28:18–20)

The mathematical formula is in the Great Commission: Don't just add disciples; multiply disciple-makers. Teach those who have chosen to follow Jesus to obey everything he commanded you.

Won't that eat up precious time? Yes, but what's the last command Jesus gave? "Make disciples." Every time one disciple teaches another disciple to make more disciples, addition gives way to multiplication.

If you want to know how the message of Jesus made it from the first century to the twenty-first century, from Israel to you, this is the answer. And if you want to know how Jesus intends to finish the job, getting the good news to the billions who have not yet heard it, look in the mirror. He wants to do it through disciples like you.

Spreadsheets rarely inspire me, but years ago I came across one that permanently changed my priorities. It compares the ministries of two individuals—one an evangelist who leads one person to Christ *per day*, the other a disciple-maker who leads one person to Christ *per year*, then invests the rest of that year teaching that new Christian to obey everything Jesus commanded. Notice how many new Christians each strategy yields over time.[2]

| Year | Evangelist | Discipler |
|------|-----------|-----------|
| 1 | 365 | 2 |
| 2 | 730 | 4 |
| 3 | 1095 | 8 |
| 4 | 1460 | 16 |
| 5 | 1825 | 32 |
| 6 | 2190 | 64 |
| 7 | 2555 | 128 |
| 8 | 2920 | 256 |
| 9 | 3285 | 512 |
| 10 | 3650 | 1024 |
| 11 | 4015 | 2048 |
| 12 | 4380 | 4096 |
| 13 | 4745 | 8192 |
| 14 | 5110 | 16,384 |
| 15 | 5475 | 32,768 |
| 16 | 5840 | 65,536 |
| 17 | 6205 | 131,072 |
| 18 | 6570 | 262,144 |
| 19 | 6935 | 524,288 |
| 20 | 7300 | 1,048,576 |
| 21 | 7665 | 2,097,152 |
| 22 | 8030 | 4,194,304 |
| 23 | 8395 | 8,388,608 |
| 24 | 8760 | 16,777,216 |
| 25 | 9125 | 33,554,432 |

| Year | Evangelist | Discipler |
|------|-----------|-----------|
| 26 | 9490 | 67,108,864 |
| 27 | 9855 | 134,217,728 |
| 28 | 10,220 | 268,435,456 |
| 29 | 10,585 | 536,870,912 |
| 30 | 10,950 | 1,073,741,824 |
| 31 | 11,315 | 2,147,483,648 |
| 32 | 11,680 | 4,294,967,296 |
| 33 | 12,045 | 8,589,934,592 |

Do you see it? If the whole church obeyed the Great Commission fully, we could reach the entire world *in this generation*. So why are there still so many people on this planet who have never heard the good news? Because a chain is only as strong as its weakest link. Every time a disciple ignores the Great Commission, a bridge between Jesus and countless lost people collapses.

I know you don't want that. Neither does Jesus. That's why he has given you everything you need to be a successful multiplier of disciples.

## Why You Can Do It

First, he has given you *adequate preparation*. You may say, "I'm not ready." Yes, you are. Everything he has taught you since the day you first started following him has equipped you to be a disciple-maker. And do you think it's a coincidence that you are reading this book? It's not. Jesus has been preparing you to do what he did. It has been his plan all along, not just to pour his truth into you, but to channel it through you. No matter how ill-prepared you feel, the truth is that you are ready.

133

Second, he has given you *a simple plan*. Three steps: go, baptize, teach. That's all you have to do.

First you have to *go*. Remember playing hide-and-seek as a kid? When you were "it," did you ever find anybody by staying at home base? No, you had to go in order to seek. As Christians, we would rather stay where we are and have lost people come to us. But that's not the way disciple-making works. We have to venture out of our comfort zone.

For the first year of my Christian life, I was verbal about my faith with one category of people: strangers. But I was silent among those I loved the most. Among my family and friends, the person I most wanted *not* to talk to about Jesus was my brother, Mike—because he and I had grown up making fun of Christians. I couldn't bear the thought of admitting to him that I had become one.

And yet I wanted him to have eternal life. Ever so slowly, love cast out fear. The day came when I knew I had to talk to Mike about Jesus. He and Lisa had been married just a few months, and I was driving to their apartment to visit them when the Spirit of God, who had been whispering to me about sharing my faith with them, all but shouted to me, "Today is the day." I felt like throwing up, I was so scared.

My heart was beating out of my chest as I walked down the corridor toward their apartment. I took a deep breath and rang the doorbell. Lisa answered. She said that Mike was not home from work yet, so I felt a temporary reprieve. But then she asked me one of those what-must-I-do-to-be-saved questions that made me realize the Lord had me cornered. So in fear and trembling I took out a booklet I had put in my pocket (just in case) called *The Four Spiritual Laws*. It was the tract of choice in those days, and I read it to her, word for word. To my astonishment, she put her faith in Jesus right then and there.

As soon as she finished praying, she said to me, "You've got to tell Mike about this when he gets home!"

I groaned, "I know, I know."

As soon as Mike walked in the door, Lisa said to him, "Mike, Greg has something he wants to share with you."

He looked at me suspiciously. "What?"

Gulp. I braced myself and pulled out the booklet. By sheer will, I read it to him, in monotone. It felt like an unpleasant medical procedure. All I wanted was to get it over with.

When I read the page that said we must individually receive Jesus Christ as Savior and Lord, he responded oddly. He sent me outside.

When I came back in, he said, gruffly, "Well, I did it."

"You did what?"

"I prayed that prayer in the booklet."

"You did?" I couldn't believe it.

"Uh-huh."

I said, "Well, you don't seem very happy about it."

"No, I am," he said. "It's just that I don't understand why nobody has ever told me this before."

I do. It was because he had a brother who wrestled with the Lord for a year before he did what he knew he had been commanded to do.

To whom has the Spirit of God been calling you to go? Please don't wait as long to obey as I did.

The second part of your mission is to *baptize*. This step may seem inessential, but who are we to make that judgment? Jesus said to do it. I suspect that one reason why is because there's something about going public that transforms faith from an experiment into a commitment. But whatever his reasons, Jesus ordained baptism as the means by which a person expresses faith. Not praying a prayer. Not checking a box on a card. Not raising a hand. Not walking an aisle. Just getting in the water and going under, in the name of the Father and of the Son and of the Holy Spirit.

The baptismal water is symbolic of so many things: the grave into which we bury our old life and from which we are raised to a new life (Rom. 6:4); the dressing room in which we become clothed with the righteousness of Christ (Gal. 3:27); the bathtub in which our sins are washed away (1 Peter 3:21).

When do all these changes take place? When do we die to our old life and rise to a new life? When are we clothed with Christ? When do we get a fresh start? At the moment we believe. So when should we baptize those we lead to Christ? As close as possible to the moment they believe. Read the book of Acts, and you will see that, without exception, whenever the timing of a person's baptism is mentioned, it is immediately after they put their faith in Jesus.

Who is supposed to do the baptizing? You are. Jesus did not give the Great Commission to ordained ministers but to all disciples. I attended a worship service recently where a businessman baptized his ninety-year-old mother. There she was, in the water, hair as white as her robe. He asked her if she believed that Jesus is the Son of the living God. "Yes!" she shouted in a gravelly voice. Down went her head, up came her feet, right out of the water, and the place erupted. That kind of raw obedience is what Jesus is after.

The third and final part of your job description is to *teach*. You may say, "Oh, please, let the pastor do that." But Jesus says, "No, I want you to do it."

Read Matthew 28:20 very slowly. Notice every detail.

Notice that the *goal* of teaching is not to impart knowledge but to instill obedience. Often when I hear others quote the Great Commission, they say, "Teaching them everything I have commanded you." The church does that well—we're good at making people smarter sinners[3]—but that's not what Jesus told us to do. He told us to teach them *to obey* everything he has commanded us. And the best way to do that is by example. Just by obeying Jesus you will teach newer disciples to obey him.

And don't miss the *content* of our teaching. What is it? The whole Bible? No. That's a good ultimate goal, but it is not our initial goal. Jesus commanded us to pass on to others his teachings. Never forget that a Christian is someone who follows Christ. You don't have to become an expert on all Scripture, but you do need to be a student of the Gospels. "Let *the word of Christ* dwell in you richly as you teach and admonish one another" (Col. 3:16).

Finally, don't dodge the tough stuff. Teach others to obey *everything* Jesus commanded, because—as you and I are discovering—his easy yoke and his light burden are found in his most radical teachings.

## He Lives in You

Let me guess. You feel overwhelmed. Me too. Why? Because we know we're underqualified. But that's no excuse, because Jesus supplies us with *divine power*. "Surely I am with you always," he said (Matt. 28:20). By that he didn't mean, "I'm behind you 100 percent." He meant, "Wherever you go, I go." And notice the expiration date on the promise: "To the end of the age." The end hasn't come yet, so the resurrected Jesus is with us as fully as he was with the original eleven.

A woman in my church gave my wife and me a very generous gift: two tickets to a live theater production of *The Lion King*. I was grateful for the gift, but skeptical about the show. I had already seen the movie (with my kids, of course), and I was told the musical had an identical script. *What an expensive rerun*, I thought.

But it was fascinatingly fresh. Lions, gazelles, giraffes, zebras, hyenas, and elephants were magically portrayed. But my favorite character was Zazu, the little bird that follows Simba everywhere he goes. I couldn't imagine how they were going to create a talking bird onstage. Well, they just made a puppet, and they put it in the hands of a puppeteer, who wore dark clothing and walked around onstage right behind the bird. It was the audience's job to pretend not to see the man who made the bird talk.

That's what serving Jesus is like. When he calls us to do something for him, whether it is to share his message of eternal life or to help those who embrace that message to join his ever-multiplying team of messengers, he gives us what we need to do what he wants. We may not be able to see him, but he is there, just as surely as the man is behind the bird.

So, before you set this book down, think about your relational web. There is somebody in it whom you can disciple. And when you do it, you will be making an eternal investment, not only in that person's life, but also in the life of everyone discipled by that person—and everyone discipled by those who are discipled by that person. On and on the multiplication process goes. Two billion and counting.

Don't break the chain.

# Conclusion

While I wrote this book, I read another one. It's called *Reading Jesus*, and in it, at the end of a chapter on Christ's hard sayings, Mary Gordon admits: "I would not have followed Jesus."[1] I lament her decision, but I respect her honesty. She listened to Jesus without plugging her ears, she counted the cost, and she decided his teachings were simply too disruptive to follow.

And too stringent. The chapter that begins a sentence after her admission is titled "The Problem of Perfection: Could We Live the Way He Says Even If We Wanted To?" That's a question that gnaws at me whenever I teach or write about Jesus: *Am I telling others to do what I have not done?* Because the answer is *yes*. If this book were not about what Jesus taught but about my efforts to obey those teachings, it would be more confessional than confrontational—because my apprehension of the truth exceeds my obedience to it.

But is that not the way it always is with Jesus? His teachings level us. They put us in the company of his original disciples, every last one of whom ultimately failed to follow him. But we must never forget that it was then that Jesus went to the cross. And it was there that he paid the price for our failures, suffering the fate we deserve.

If these chapters have made you more aware of your shortcomings, that is a good place to land. But it is no place to linger—because Jesus taught us not just in order to expose our deficiencies but also to beckon us to a better life. Yes, we are sinners. Thank God we have a Savior. But our Savior is also our Lord, and so the very same words that brought us to our knees have become the yoke we wear and the burden we bear. Let us press on in following Jesus, with shattered pride and desperate dependence on his Spirit, trusting that he is leading us to a life that is so much easier and so much lighter than the one we left behind.

# Acknowledgments

How do I begin to thank those who have contributed to a project that has taken half of my life to complete? Do I mention the seeds that were planted in my soul so long ago by teachers like John Grassmick, Darrell Bock, and Mark Bailey, who never tried to explain why Jesus could not possibly mean what he clearly said? Do I thank seminary classmates like Doug Schillinger and Daniel Low and Chris Regas, who fueled my passion to know Jesus and make him known? Do I acknowledge all those who have sat under my teaching at the churches I have served and have never said, "Can we please study something other than the Gospels?"

And who among the many friends I have asked to read embryonic versions of this book should I mention by name? Certainly Steve Walker, Paula Tremayne, and Glenn Wade, who have read so many drafts over the past decade they must be thanking God it's finally in print and I can't give them any more rewrites. But there have been so many others.

Do I express appreciation to Tim Riter for encouraging me to pursue my dream, and coaching me every step of the way? Do I thank Vicki Crumpton for persuading her team at Revell to take a risk on this unknown author, and for helping me to make the final product so much better than my rough draft?

And how can I put into words the depth of my gratitude to my wife, Robin, who has supported me, listened to me, and sacrificed for me for twenty years?

I can only say, to all these people and countless others who have in some way contributed to this labor of love, I thank my God every time I remember you.

# Study Guide

## Before Reading Chapter 1

Think of at least one other person with whom you might be able to study this book. (The accountability will help both of you follow Jesus more closely.)

Using a concordance, try to find every occurrence of the phrase "follow me" in the Gospels. What can you learn about Jesus from the passages in which he speaks those words?

## After Reading Chapter 1

1. Would you consider yourself a "back-row" Christian or "front-row" disciple? What keeps you from moving closer to where the action is?
2. If Jesus were to give you a nickname that describes the kind of person you are right now, what might it be? If he were to give you a name that reflects what you have

the potential to become under his influence, what would it be?

3. What is the furthest you have "traveled" outside your comfort zone to help change people's lives? What effect did the depth of your commitment have on your spiritual productivity and passion?

4. What is the one thing you are most reluctant to let go of in order to follow Jesus? What will happen if you do let it go? What will happen if you don't?

*Christ-quote to memorize:* "Come, follow me, and I will make you fishers of men" (Matt. 4:19).

## Before Reading Chapter 2

Read John 8:30–32 in at least three Bible versions, then paraphrase what Jesus says in verse 31 without using the words "hold," "abide," "teaching," "word," or "disciples."

## After Reading Chapter 2

1. Are you a Christian? If so, when and how did you become one? Are you a disciple? If so, when and how did you become one?

2. How sure are you that Jesus (as opposed to other religious leaders) is the source of truth? What gives you assurance? What causes you to doubt?

3. How would you define freedom? Which makes you feel more free—doing your own thing or obeying Jesus? Why?

4. In what areas are you in bondage because of disobedience to Jesus? What practical steps can you take to experience the freedom Jesus wants to give you?

*Christ-quote to memorize:* "If you hold to my teaching, you are really my disciples" (John 8:31).

## Before Reading Chapter 3

Read John 8:31–51 in a literal translation such as the English Standard Version, the New American Standard Bible, or the New King James Version. Highlight every occurrence of the term "word." How do the verses that include "word" illuminate each other?

## After Reading Chapter 3

1. What is the difference between counterfeit faith and genuine faith, according to Jesus?
2. Do you think the terms "Christian" and "disciple" are synonymous? Why or why not? What Scriptures support your view? What Scriptures challenge your view?
3. How would you explain John 8:51 to a person who stubbornly—and rightly—defends the doctrine of salvation by faith alone?
4. In what area of your life is your "faith" in Jesus's teaching contradicted by your disobedience to it? How can you close the gap?

*Christ-quote to memorize:* "I tell you the truth, if anyone keeps my word, he will never see death" (John 8:51).

## Before Reading Chapter 4

Read Matthew 10:37 and Luke 14:26, then define the word "hate" as Jesus used it.

## After Reading Chapter 4

1. What three people (other than Jesus) do you love the most? Do you love Jesus more or less than them? How do you know?
2. At what forks in the road of your Christian life have you been forced to "hate" either Jesus or someone else you loved? Whom did you "love"? What were the benefits and consequences of your choice?
3. Is there anyone in your life who, right now, is in any way vying with Jesus for your loyalty? What must you do to follow Jesus wholeheartedly?

*Christ-quote to memorize:* "If anyone comes to me and does not hate his father and mother, his wife and children, his brothers and sisters—yes, even his own life—he cannot be my disciple" (Luke 14:26).

## Before Reading Chapter 5

Read Luke 9:23 and Luke 14:27 in at least two translations. Write down what you think it means to carry your cross.

## After Reading Chapter 5

1. How has your understanding of cross-carrying been tweaked or reinforced by what you read in this chapter?
2. What relevance does Luke 14:27 have to those of us who do not live in places where following Jesus is a life-threatening commitment?
3. When have you had to pay a price for your allegiance to Jesus? When have you downplayed your faith in him to avoid paying a price?

*Christ-quote to memorize:* "If anyone would come after me, he must deny himself and take up his cross daily and follow me" (Luke 9:23).

## Before Reading Chapter 6

Read Luke 9:23–26. Compare the cost of discipleship with the cost of non-discipleship.

## After Reading Chapter 6

1. What do you think it means to be ashamed of Jesus? What do you think it means for him to be ashamed of you? (Read Luke 12:8–9; 2 Timothy 2:12; and Revelation 3:5 for clues.)
2. What does our courage, or our cowardice, reveal about our faith?
3. Realistically, what price might you have to pay for being an outspoken follower of Jesus? The next time you are

tempted to distance yourself from him, how will you overcome that temptation?

*Christ-quote to memorize:* "Whoever acknowledges me before men, I will also acknowledge him before my Father in heaven" (Matt. 10:32).

## Before Reading Chapter 7

Read Luke 14:33 in multiple translations. What other New Testament passages tell disciples what to do with their wealth? How do the pieces fit together?

## After Reading Chapter 7

1. Paraphrase Luke 14:33 without using the word "disciple." What is Jesus saying we cannot do without giving up our possessions?
2. Do you think we have to give away our possessions in order to give them up? If not, what is Jesus asking us to do? How do you know if you have done it?
3. Which of your possessions are you most reluctant to relinquish? Why? How can you be a faithful steward of that possession?
4. What is the biggest financial sacrifice you have ever made for Jesus? How did the cost compare with the reward?

*Christ-quote to memorize:* "Any of you who does not give up everything he has cannot be my disciple" (Luke 14:33).

## Before Reading Chapter 8

Read John 13:34–35, and write down at least ten observations about the passage. (Don't try to interpret it yet, just record the details you notice.)

## After Reading Chapter 8

1. If you can remember a time in your life when you were apathetic about Jesus, why was that the case? Who or what piqued your interest?
2. If we want all people to know that we are Christ's disciples, whom must we love more—co-disciples or non-disciples? Why?
3. What are some ways you have seen the forces of evil keep Christians from loving one another? What were the consequences?
4. What are some practical ways that you can love other Christians this week in such a way that non-Christians see it?

*Christ-quote to memorize:* "By this everyone will know that you are my disciples, if you love one another" (John 13:35 TNIV).

## Before Reading Chapter 9

Read John 13:1–17. Try to imagine what you would have seen and felt if you were in the upper room. How would you summarize Jesus's teaching in verses 12–17?

## After Reading Chapter 9

1. What does John 13:1–11 teach you about love that the cross does not?
2. What adjectives would you use to describe Christlike love, based on this scene? Which of those adjectives is most challenging to you personally? Why?
3. From whom in the body of Christ are you most tempted to withhold love? Why shouldn't you?
4. What are some of the most "hands-on" ways other Christians have loved you? What is something practical you can do for a fellow disciple within the next seventy-two hours?

*Christ-quote to memorize:* "Now that I, your Lord and Teacher, have washed your feet, you also should wash one another's feet" (John 13:14).

## Before Reading Chapter 10

Using a concordance, find every occurrence of the word "fruit" in the Gospel of John. What does the fruit symbolize in each passage?

## After Reading Chapter 10

1. Would you consider yourself a fruitful Christian? Why or why not?
2. Who are some people you have influenced spiritually? How? Who are some people you have not yet influenced spiritually but would like to?

3. Make your best argument for being ill-equipped to lead others to Christ. Then refute that argument with what you learned from John 15:1–8.
4. What is the most important thing you can do to help others live forever? (Don't say it with biblical language; put it in your own words.)

*Christ-quote to memorize:* "This is to my Father's glory, that you bear much fruit, showing yourselves to be my disciples" (John 15:8).

## Before Reading Chapter 11

Read John 15:4–5. If a brand-new Christian were to ask you what it means to abide in Christ—and how to do it—what would you say?

## After Reading Chapter 11

1. What insights do the following passages give you about what it means to abide in Christ?
   John 6:56
   John 15:10
   John 15:12
   1 John 2:24
   1 John 3:24
   1 John 4:15
2. When have you tried, and failed, to serve the Lord in your own strength? When have you relied completely on him, with supernatural results?

3. How can the truth of John 15:5 help you with the challenges of the discipleship passages you have studied in chapters 1–11?

*Christ-quote to memorize:* "I am the vine; you are the branches. If you remain in me and I in you, you will bear much fruit; apart from me you can do nothing" (John 15:5 TNIV).

## Before Reading Chapter 12

List as many passages from the Gospels as you can that help answer this question: Does Jesus expect every disciple to share their faith?

## After Reading Chapter 12

1. What passage of Scripture best encapsulates Christ's mission in life? Combine that passage with Luke 6:40. What is your mission in life?
2. How much of the Great Commission applies to only the original eleven disciples, and how much of it applies to us?
3. What different faith-sharing expectations do you think Jesus has for non-evangelists than he does for those who have the gift of evangelism? What does he expect of you?

*Christ-quote to memorize:* "For the Son of Man came to seek and to save what was lost" (Luke 19:10).

## Before Reading Chapter 13

Read Matthew 28:18–20, and write down as many truths as you can find.

## After Reading Chapter 13

1. In what ways are you going, baptizing, and teaching right now? Which part of your job description are you fulfilling? Which part aren't you fulfilling?
2. What are your most glaring liabilities as a disciple-maker? What assets does Jesus have to compensate for those liabilities?
3. What are some of the most important truths you learned from this study?
4. Who are three people you could "teach" the study you have just completed? How can you translate good intentions into action?

*Christ-quote to memorize:* "Go and make disciples of all nations, baptizing them in the name of the Father and of the Son and of the Holy Spirit, and teaching them to obey everything I have commanded you" (Matt. 28:19–20).

# Notes

### Chapter 3  Minimum Requirement

1. The apostle Paul teaches the very same truth, albeit using different terminology—most prominently, "flesh" and "Spirit." Read his Epistles carefully, and you will see that his teaching on the relationship between faith and obedience is in perfect harmony with the teaching of Jesus.

### Chapter 4  Love/Hate

1. G. Campbell Morgan, *Studies in the Four Gospels: The Gospel according to Luke* (New York: Fleming H. Revell, 1927), 176.

2. I am aware that Jesus may well have spoken Aramaic, which does not have multiple words for love as the Greek language does. But there was something in the way Jesus spoke these words that caused Matthew, under the inspiration of the Holy Spirit, to choose the verb *phileo* rather than the far more common *agapao*.

### Chapter 5  Cross Walk

1. Two of Lt. Christian's cell mates, John McCain and Leo Thorsness, have told this story, with minor differences in detail, in speeches that are posted on multiple websites, including YouTube (search for "The Mike Christian Story").

2. Are you wondering what happened to my friend? Good news: He didn't deny Christ, and he didn't die.

3. For statistical information on worldwide Christian martyrdom, see http://ockenga.gordonconwell.edu/ockenga/globalchristianity/gd/gd16 .pdf.

4. Although there is widespread agreement among Christian historians that ten of the eleven apostles died as martyrs, ancient sources sometimes disagree on the details. See William Steuart McBirnie, *The Search for the Twelve Apostles* (Wheaton: Tyndale, 2008) for a comprehensive treatment on this subject.

5. John White, *The Cost of Commitment* (Downers Grove, IL: InterVarsity, 1976), 31–32.

6. "Memorials: The Wall's Mistaken Men," *Time*, November 23, 1987.

### Chapter 6 The Cost of Non-Discipleship

1. Again, as in Matthew 10:37, the Spirit-inspired Gospel writer chose a Greek translation that accurately reflected the nuance of the words Jesus spoke in Aramaic. Some have argued that the use of two different Greek verbs is nothing more than a stylistic variation, but I am compelled by the details of the text to conclude that John's choice of words was precise and significant.

2. Origen (185–254) reported that "Peter was crucified at Rome with his head downwards, as he himself had desired to suffer."

### Chapter 8 Credibility Gap

1. There is abundant information on the internet about Dr. Semmelweis, including these articles: Christa Colyer, "Childbed Fever: A Nineteenth-Century Mystery," October 27, 2003, http://www.sciencecases.org/childbed_fever/childbed_fever.asp; Semmelweis Society International, "Dr. Semmelweis," http://www.semmelweis.org/about/dr-semmelweis-biography/; Mary Bellis, "History of Antiseptics," About.com, http://inventors.about.com/library/inventors/blantisceptics.htm; Ole Daniel Enersen, "Ignaz Philipp Semmelweis," WhoNamedIt.com, 2010, http://www.whonamedit.com/doctor.cfm/354.html.

### Chapter 9 Down and Dirty

1. William Barclay, *The Gospel of John* (Louisville: Westminster John Knox Press, 2001), 161.

2. Here and in other parts of the book, I have used fictitious names when it seems appropriate to protect someone's identity.

3. Quoted by Darryl Bell in "To Illustrate," *Leadership* 5, no. 4 (Fall 1984), available online at http://www.christianitytoday.com/le/1984/fall/84l4046.html?start=3.

### Chapter 11  Abiding for Dummies

1. Andrew Murray, *Abide in Christ* (New Kensington, PA: Whitaker House, 1979), 117–18, 131–32.

2. Corrie Ten Boom, "I'm Still Learning to Forgive," *Guideposts*, November 1972.

### Chapter 12  Search and Rescue

1. From a message at the 2002 Willow Creek Small Group Conference. The story of the Massachusetts Humane Society is also told by Ortberg in *Everybody's Normal till You Get to Know Them* (Grand Rapids: Zondervan, 2003), 88–89.

2. By this I mean that there is only one passage I am aware of in the Gospels in which Jesus *commands* all disciples to make more disciples. Another significant passage to think deeply about is Luke 6:40, where Jesus said, "A student [*mathetes*] is not above his teacher, but everyone who is fully trained will be like his teacher." One implication of that truth is that, as we mature as disciples of Jesus, we will adopt his life mission, which was to seek and to save what was lost.

### Chapter 13  The Power of One

1. *Shrek the Third*, DVD, directed by Chris Miller and Raman Hui (Hollywood, CA: Paramount Home Video/Dreamworks, 2007).

2. Keith Phillips, *The Making of a Disciple* (Old Tappan, NJ: Revell, 1981), 23.

3. This was one of the many memorable phrases I heard from Dr. Howard Hendricks, one of my professors at Dallas Theological Seminary.

### Conclusion

1. Mary Gordon, *Reading Jesus* (New York: Pantheon Books, 2009), 124.

**Greg Sidders** (ThM, Dallas Theological Seminary) is a former journalist and the pastor of White Pine Community Church in Cumberland, Maine. He and his wife, Robin, have three sons. He blogs at www.gregsidders.com.